Choosing a

DIVORCE

MEDIATOR

Also by Diane Neumann

DIVORCE MEDIATION:
How to Cut the Cost
and Stress of Divorce

Choosing a

DIVORCE

MEDIATOR

A Guide to Help

Divorcing Couples Find

a Competent Mediator

DIANE NEUMANN

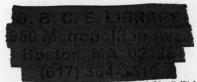
AN OWL BOOK

HENRY HOLT AND COMPANY / NEW YORK

Henry Holt and Company, Inc.
Publishers since 1866
115 West 18th Street
New York, New York 10011

Henry Holt® is a registered
trademark of Henry Holt and Company, Inc.

Published in Canada by Fitzhenry & Whiteside Ltd.,
195 Allstate Parkway, Markham, Ontario L3R 4T8.

Library of Congress Cataloging-in-Publication Data
Neumann, Diane.
Choosing a divorce mediator/Diane Neumann.
p.   cm.
"An Owl book."
Includes index.
1. Divorce mediation—United States.   2. Divorce—Law
and legislation—United States—Popular works.   I. Title.
HQ834. N467   1996   96-24891
306.89—dc20   CIP
ISBN 0-8050-4762-X

Henry Holt books are available for special
promotions and premiums. For details contact:
Director, Special Markets.

First Owl Book Edition—1996
Designed by Victoria Hartman

Printed in the United States of America
All first editions are printed on acid-free paper.∞
1 2 3 4 5 6 7 8 9 10

To my parents,
Paul and Nancy Patania

Contents

Acknowledgments

I want to thank Shel, Brian, and Stacey for their continued support; my agent, Diana Finch; and especially my editor, Cynthia Vartan. Most of all, however, I want to thank all of my mediation clients for showing me the meaning of character, even while in the throes of divorce.

Choosing a

DIVORCE

MEDIATOR

Introduction

Divorce. The picture years ago was this: Divorcing men and women hiring cutthroat lawyers to fight their battles in divorce court. Divorce lawyers inciting their clients to litigate. Packed courts filled with lies and counterlies. Embattled parents using children as custody trophies. Men and women beginning their new lives bitter and vengeful. And their children, the real victims of the divorce court battles, learning to cope with the changes.

Many people, from divorcing couples to the professionals who work with them, have begun to realize that hiring adversarial lawyers to do battle with a spouse only serves to promote expensive litigation, incur health-risking stress, heighten the bitterness, and create lifelong scars. More than ever, we realize that people need the kind of assistance that will not exacerbate the problems of divorce, as in the old model, but rather the help to reach a fair agreement and, just as important, allow family members to get on with their lives.

During the 1980s, our cultural attitude toward divorce changed profoundly. Where once society condemned divorced people, we began to find ways to help them: Churches, originally the leaders in opposing divorce, started to provide support groups; community centers offered informative programs for those contemplating divorce; and schools organized groups for children whose parents were divorcing. Therapists began to talk about the stages of the process, authors wrote books describing healthy ways to divorce, and even lawyers gave second thought to encouraging their clients to wage destructive custody battles.

We now recognize that there is a better way to reach a divorce settlement—through a process called mediation. In the 1990s, couples are turning to mediators as a means of reducing the terrible financial and emotional costs of divorce. Though divorce remains a difficult process, the use of mediation provides a civilized approach to the issues facing those who are ending their relationship as husband and wife. And the challenge now is finding a good mediator.

I began as a mediator in January 1981. Up until that time, I was in private practice as a therapist, but I wanted to have the same kind of telephone listing for my mediation practice as I had as a therapist. I called my local Yellow Pages advertising department to place a new ad, with a listing for my new occupation—divorce mediator.

"What in the world is a . . . divorce *meditator?*" the representative asked incredulously.

"It's a mediator," I corrected (one of those early times in a stream of hundreds, maybe thousands, of times of correcting that word), and gave a brief description of the mediation process.

"Seems like a good idea to me. I could've used you for my divorce. It was a mess. But," he added, "I can't give you a listing for that."

"Why not?"

"Because there is no listing for 'mediator.' There's just no such category," he answered.

Five years later, however, the Yellow Pages finally agreed to list "Mediation Services." Almost immediately, several other names appeared under the listing, and just as suddenly, the listing appeared in many other directories. Look in the Yellow Pages of your phone book, and you'll see the problem of choosing the right one for you.

Why is it so difficult to find a good divorce mediator? There are three primary reasons: Divorce mediation is a new profession, just twenty years old. There is either no or insufficient licensing or regulating of the qualifications for who can be a mediator. And there is a lack of recognizable indicators of mediator competence.

Although the profession of divorce mediation is very young, other kinds of mediation have existed for some time. Foremost among them is labor mediation, in which a third party provides a reasonable forum to resolve labor-management disputes while maintaining the ongoing relationship between the workers and managers. Mediation worked extremely well and is used in other "sensitive" areas, such as international conflict. Divorce, however, was considered fair game for bitter and expensive court litigation. The relationship between a divorcing man and woman—even those who had young children—was not considered a "sensitive" relationship that would benefit by a more humane dispute resolution process. Only when divorcing individuals got fed up with the tremendous expense and turmoil of the old system did the idea of divorce mediation take root.

The first divorce mediator was retired lawyer turned psychotherapist, O. J. Coogler, whose successful work with teens and their parents convinced him that conflict between angry family members could be resolved with a process known as mediation. Coogler used the process with his divorcing clients, with immense success. Now, there was a better way. The year was 1976, and the field of divorce mediation was born.

Twenty years is simply not enough time for a profession to create standards for itself—to say "this is what a mediator does" or "just this and nothing else," or "a mediator should do all of this" or "a mediator never does that." There is a lot of very different mediation practice out there, and I don't just mean in personal style. Differences in actual practice, from methods of mediation to the type of final divorce document created, can vary widely.

A second problem is that mediators are not licensed in the same way as other divorce professionals. This is a critical difference. Divorce lawyers, for example, must be licensed by the state in which they practice and in order to be licensed, they must meet stringent criteria. In virtually every state, with the exception of Vermont, where one may practice law without attending law school, a lawyer must graduate from an approved law school, which means three years of rigorous full-time education. But education is only part of the story. The state further mandates that the law school graduate must sit for that most formidable of tests—the bar exam. Professionals in the field of mental health have similar requirements in order to be licensed. A licensed therapist, psychologist, or psychiatrist must achieve specific educational requirements and, in addition, must fulfill a period known as supervision or internship, during which the new graduate works under the direction of an experienced practitioner.

It is a very different case with the profession of mediation. In most states, anyone can hang out a shingle proclaiming him- or herself a mediator.

Although a small number of states provide for the certification of mediators—a step well below the rigorous requirements for licensing—the vast majority of states do not. But let me be clear: Certification does not mean a mediator is competent. What it does mean is that the mediator has met minimum criteria. However, the concern with mediator certification today is that the required criteria are very low. Even the Academy of Family Mediators, a national organization comprised primarily of private divorce mediators, does not certify mediators (which it could do and is contemplating). The Academy does offer two levels of membership: a General Member, which just means having paid a fee, or a Practitioner Member, which currently requires only sixty hours of mediation training and one hundred hours of mediation experience. In comparison, this sixty-hour requirement is much lower than some states' training require-ments to license hair dressers or plumbers.

Many divorce professionals are dismayed by the lack of re-quirements for divorce mediators. It is hoped that this situation will be addressed soon and that the appropriate requirements will emerge. Until that time, however, and until there are rec-ognizable indicators of a mediator's competence (knowledge of divorce law, for instance), divorcing couples need guidelines to help choose a mediator who is both competent and the right one for them.

In the pages that follow, I offer those guidelines. After an overview of the mediation process itself and a discussion of what types of marital disputes are appropriate and inappropriate for mediation, I go into how to assess your own needs to determine what skills and expertise you will want your mediator to have. (For instance, if you have children, you will want someone with a background in child development and a knowledge of local court practices regarding custody. If you own a house, you will want your mediator to have expertise in real estate transactions and tax consequences.) I then suggest ways to generate the names of potential mediators and the best way to approach them. I discuss the questions you should ask during your initial interviews, such as how long they have been mediating, what training they have, do they provide a free introductory session, and so forth. I discuss the unavoidable question—the gender of the mediator, and why that makes a difference—and, finally, whether you will eventually need a lawyer.

I hope that this book will show how vital it is to choose your mediator carefully—one who is both competent and right for your specific needs. It will be well worth the time and effort in-volved to ensure that you and your spouse are satisfied with the results of your mediation.

1

Considering Divorce Mediation

Mediation can save you a lot of money and misery. If you are not convinced, do two things for yourself: First, read this book. Second, talk to divorced people who did *not* use mediation—as many as you can. Ask questions and most of all, listen. Chances are good that the stories you hear will make you run, not walk, to your nearest divorce mediator. However, the nearest mediator may not be the one for you. Even if you have already contacted a mediator, this book will help you decide whether you have made the right choice. If you discover that you have not, it is not too late to switch.

Mediation provides a place to make informed decisions and a mediator helps you gather the relevant information you need to make those decisions. This is why mediated agreements last, whereas divorce agreements negotiated by divorce lawyers so often end up with the parties back in court. Study after study has concluded that a minimum of 50 percent of all divorced people are back in court within one year of their divorce on a contempt, which occurs when a person does not follow a court order and the other party brings a court action, or a modification, which happens when one of the divorced persons brings a court action to change a prior court order. This percentage figure is rarely disputed. In fact, professionals who work in the divorce field believe it is significantly higher. When you understand how the two worlds work—mediation versus the adversarial courts— it will be clearer how one method so often leads to a fair resolution, while the other leads to a bitter court battle.

As you consider mediation, it helps to have a clear understanding of the process. In providing an overview, I use my practice as the example, since I know it best and understand how it works. I have had a private mediation practice in Framingham, Massachusetts, since January 1981. In addition to myself, I have a panel of four trained and experienced mediators. The majority of our work is comprehensive divorce mediation. We all follow the same procedure.

Upon a first call from a potential client, our assistant makes two inquiries. First, she asks whether the caller would like to receive a free divorce mediation information packet (sent in an envelope which does not have the word *divorce* on it—a minor point, yet one that may be important to a client). Second, she asks if the caller wants to talk to a mediator. If the response is yes, a mediator then describes the mediation process and answers the caller's questions. The mediator, of course, cannot discuss any of the specifics of the situation with the caller, as mediators are meant to be impartial and may hear such information only during a joint session, with both clients present.

Following the initial call, the caller's spouse also may phone to speak with the mediator, but in our office, this does not occur often. At some point, one of the couple calls back to set up an appointment, scheduled for ninety minutes. The first half hour is a free, introductory session; the next hour is optional. If the couple chooses to go ahead with the mediation, the time has been reserved for them. However, if either or both of them does not want to use the optional hour, the appointment ends, and there is no charge.

The purpose of this introductory session is for the mediator to describe the process to the prospective clients. I encourage each person to ask questions, but frequently the couple will say something along the lines of "I don't know what to ask." Be assured that you will know what to ask after reading this book.

During this session, I review the basic process, such as the average length of a session (ninety minutes), the average number of sessions for a couple with minor children and a house or a condo (five after that first appointment), and the fees charged (an hourly rate, with no retainer required). I list all of the charges and discuss cancellations and appointment changes. (This is an area that you should understand clearly; chapter 7 takes a longer look at fees and charges.)

The mediator gives each person a copy of the mediation contract to take home to review, so if there are any questions, there will be time to consult with an attorney before signing. The contract will be signed at the start of the next session. I explain the contract by saying that it is written in English instead of legalese, however, *it is a legally binding contract.* If you are uneasy about signing such a contract for any reason, you should consult with an independent lawyer and bring your concerns to the mediator. Remember, every professional should be willing to explain to you the terms of a proposed contract. Do not hesitate to ask for explanations and charges.

Each mediation client must disclose all of her or his income, assets, and liability. Most clients are well aware of this requirement. Mediators differ as to how much documentation is required. Our office requires documentation, so that each person is satisfied that his or her spouse has been forthright at the negotiation table. Another area that a mediator should discuss with you is confidentiality. In my state, Massachusetts, the law provides for complete confidentiality from the court of the mediation process. This means that neither the mediator nor her notes can be subpoenaed into court to testify or give evidence for or against her client(s). Be sure to ask your mediator if your state has a confidentiality law for mediators and exactly what the law means.

A good mediator reminds clients that mediation is voluntary. She should impress upon you that a mediator is not a judge or an arbitrator, and that she cannot make any decisions for you. All decisions will be made by the couple. Some mediators may advise you to consult with an independent attorney. In fact, a number of mediators require each client to have a consulting attorney. Our office doesn't, and I think that this requirement is more common among nonattorney mediators. No mediator should attempt to minimize your right to consult with a lawyer.

The more information you receive from your mediator, the more satisfied you will feel and the better prepared you will be. At this point in time, you should feel satisfied with the mediator's qualifications if you are to continue with the process. The following chapters will outline the guidelines of a good mediator.

In the next session, I begin by asking for specific information concerning each client's financial situation, with questions along these lines: What is your salary? Do you receive bonus income? Do you have a pension plan? If so, do you know how much is in the plan? Not only does this provide me with the necessary information, but it enables me to find out the financial expertise of each client, thereby avoiding unfair agreements down the road.

Next, I describe the relevant aspects of separation and divorce. Clients generally ask a lot of questions in this area, such as "What is a legal separation?" or "Are there different kinds of divorce?" and the most frequently asked, "What is the waiting period for a divorce?" Then I point out the documents required for divorce, such as the certified copy of their marriage certificate. Even though it is the first session, it is not too early to let clients know that they need this certificate, as it may involve a lengthy wait to obtain it if they were married in a distant location.

For clients who have minor children, we have a child custody session. I begin by finding out the present parenting arrangements, then determine the arrangement each person wishes. If a couple's wants are unrealistic, or if they differ from each other, a mediator will help the clients resolve their disagreements, as well as explain the applicable state laws concerning legal and physical custody.

A small number of states are now writing laws without the words *custody* and *visitation* because of their negative connotations, though the majority of states still use these words. The mediators I know do not use either of these terms in discussing a parenting plan, employing them only when necessary. Don't ignore the language your mediator uses. Remember, you have a right to quality mediation. Someone who uses inappropriate, careless, or negative words may not be the mediator for you.

There is a lot of information available concerning the parenting of children of divorcing couples. I emphasize that the most important criterion for the adjustment of a child is the degree of conflict between the parents. The greater the degree of conflict, the greater the problems for the child. Parents want as much information as possible to help their child minimize the emotional trauma of the divorce. For those mediators who do not have a background in developmental stages or other necessary children's issues, the clients may be referred to a professional with expertise in this area.

The focus of the next session is child support. It begins with a review of each person's expense sheet. Mediators call these forms budgets, but don't let the word scare you. Budgets are actually expense forms, which may include your present or future expenses, depending on the specifics of the situation. Expense forms are an invaluable tool for examining important financial matters ahead.

Over the last few years—in response to federal dictate—every state has implemented legal child support guidelines. However, these guidelines differ from state to state. Some states allow parents to disregard the guidelines if there are good reasons to do so, while other states do not. Even if parents do not intend to follow the guidelines, and assuming they reside in a state where this is possible, the judge will still expect the clients to be aware of these guidelines, and mediators can help clients to understand them.

Many child support decisions are involved in the typical mediated divorce agreement: the amount of monetary support; whether this amount changes over the years; if it does change, the criteria to be used; and, the most difficult decision, the duration of the payments. Most clients want to be able to renegotiate child support payments between themselves or with the help of a mediator so that, in the event of unemployment, they need not go to court.

The final topic in this session, if applicable, is the payment of a child's college expenses. Parents vary on their ability and desire to legally obligate themselves to pay for college. Once again, even though mediation clients have wide discretion to make their own decisions, most want to know if there is a legal obligation for a parent to contribute to the expenses of their college-age children. Some states require divorced parents to pay for such expenses, others do not. More than one client has angrily complained that it doesn't seem fair for the law to force a divorced parent to pay for college when it doesn't force a married parent to pay for it—that is, a married parent usually cannot sue his or her spouse for money to pay for college, but in divorce, the spouse *can* do so. Clients should also be made aware of the tax consequences of child support. Taxes are not only a complex area but are part and parcel of a divorce agreement. Unfortunately, not all mediators are familiar with this difficult area.

All clients participate in the property division session. Our office provides clients with the applicable state laws on that subject. We begin with real estate, specifically the marital house or condo. Invariably, this session is a difficult one as clients grapple with the inevitable question, Who gets the house? In order to help clients make a good decision in this area, we need specific information, such as the fair market value of the property. You will also need to provide debt information on the property, such as the mortgage, equity line, and any liens. This subject often makes for hard choices: whether to sell the house, own it jointly, or have one person keep it. And at some point during this session, I explain everyone's favorite topic, capital gains tax!

At the assets/liabilities session, what is discussed depends on the specific financial situation of the divorcing couple. Assets are the items a person owns, and includes pensions, retirement accounts, stocks, bonds, vehicles, employment and self-employment plans (pension plans, 401k plans, stock options, insurance plans), bank accounts, investments, and apartment or house contents. Some assets that are not so common are closely held corporations, trusts, valuable collections, and antiques. Generally, in divorce settlements, assets must have a fair market value. Liability is the opposite of the asset coin: credit card debt, car loans and leases, school loans, IOU's, and the like.

A topic with the power to create incredible bitterness in the adversary system—and that all agree represents something other than the item itself—is the division of the contents in the residence. Mediators call this contents division; divorce lawyers disparagingly refer to it as the pots and pans issue. A significant number of our mediation clients are able to divide most or all of the contents themselves, though it is not easy to allocate items such as children's photos. Mediators can be especially helpful in this area by suggesting ways to accomplish this in the least painful manner.

After agreeing on which person is responsible for which debts, we discuss insurance and the availability and payment of health and/or dental insurance for each client and child. In many states, an ex-spouse may legally continue his or her coverage through his or her former spouse's health insurance plan. This is an increasingly important area with complex state and federal laws that will directly affect your pocketbook. In many states, life insurance is not required to be included in a divorce settlement, yet this is an important area if there are minor children or other financial obligations from one or both parents.

Some divorce agreements also include disability insurance. Two optional mediator sessions remain, one on alimony and the other called the final divorce session.

Alimony may not be a topic for all clients, but if it is part of the settlement negotiation, it is typically a highly charged topic. The tax consequences to both husband and wife are extremely complex, and if the mediator does not have a considerable degree of expertise in the area of taxes, it will be money well spent to consult a tax expert.

Filing for your own divorce is called *pro se,* Latin for "do it yourself." *Pro se* clients will go to court on their own, without attorneys. The majority of my clients file on their own and, therefore, attend the final divorce session. (Filing for your own divorce is common in most states, rare in others, and unheard of in some. Ask your mediator about the law in your state.) The purpose of the last session is to sign forms and documents and to prepare for the court process. And last, we provide free time at the end of the session for clients to comment on the mediation process.

Some people assume that mediation means compromise. It doesn't. In fact, people in mediation are more apt to get the settlement they want because they are actively involved in the decision making, rather than stating their position through their respective lawyers. Indeed, disagreements are a routine part of the mediation process. Though they may seem difficult to resolve, they can be successfully settled with a good mediator. However, both husband and wife must agreed to use the mediation process and, unfortunately, it is not unusual for either to be reluctant to see a mediator. If this poses a problem, chapter 3 discusses how to get your spouse to try mediation.

2

Is Mediation for Everyone?

The benefits of mediation, both financial and psychological, are endless, but you may feel that you and your spouse don't fit the picture of who belongs in mediation. In some instances, couples have a legitimate concern, but most are needlessly worried. Some assume, for instance, that they must agree on everything in advance and harbor no anger. These couples, if they existed, would certainly be candidates for mediation, but they do not resemble typical mediation clients. However, for some couples mediation is not appropriate, and I will discuss these later in the chapter. First, I'll describe some common situations that cause some couples to wonder whether mediation is possible.

Let me assure you that you *can* mediate when the following situations exist:

1. Tax fudging
2. Asset dispute
3. Affairs
4. Lack of communication
5. Child custody disputes
6. Leaving the marital residence disputes
7. Lawyers already hired

8. Already divorced
9. Substance abuse

1. TAX FUDGING:
Chuck and Jane were in their mid-thirties, with two young children, ages five and seven. He was self-employed as a computer consultant, and she worked part-time as a telemarketer. During the second mediation session, Jane said she was worried that Chuck had been less than truthful on the business section of his tax return. Since all clients are required to provide copies of their tax returns, I reviewed his business tax form, Schedule C, with the couple. First, I explained the form, then reviewed each business entry to see if both were satisfied with it. Each was. However, when we got to the car expenses, Jane pointed out that the business expense included personal miles that Chuck drove in his car. "It's not fair. It's not all business. I don't get to write off my personal travel expenses," she said. She asked how much Chuck deducted for mileage, and I pointed out that he deducted $5,340. Jane said that she thought the business expense was more like half that amount. It was up to Chuck to explain the inclusion of personal miles in business use or to document all of the miles as business use. After some discussion, he agreed to adjust the deduction from $5,340 to $2,670 for the purpose of their negotiations.

The question that Jane had to address was whether she was willing to understand the business deductions involved. The mediator helped with this. Let me add that, in mediation, the client must be assured that her spouse will accurately provide her with his actual income.

2. ASSET DISPUTE:
A common asset dispute often occurs when one person thinks that the item in question is one's own individual asset while the spouse believes it is a marital asset. Early one morning, for example, a man called to inquire whether mediation was possible since he and his wife were having an angry disagreement about

a piece of land he inherited from his father. He said, "I know it's mine, but she thinks it's both of ours." This kind of dispute is exactly the type of conflict for which mediation is intended.

Let me offer another example. Paul and Nancy had been married for ten years. It was a first marriage for him and a second for her. They entered the mediation room engrossed in an argument over their house. During the session, Nancy explained that she had received the house as her share of the assets upon her divorce from her first husband. Paul, however, felt that the important issue was that he had paid the mortgage for the entire ten years of their marriage. Nancy believed that the house was hers, while Paul strongly believed that the house was now a marital asset. This was a good dispute to resolve in mediation. They had each consulted with a lawyer who, of course, supported their respective positions: Her lawyer confirmed that it was a separate asset, while his lawyer confirmed it was a marital asset. During mediation, they negotiated a settlement in which Nancy bought out Paul's interest for less than one-half of the equity—a little more than she wanted to pay, and a little less than he wanted to receive. Most people who come to my office have serious disagreements concerning division of assets. It's my job to help them to resolve these conflicts.

3. AFFAIRS:

It's amazing to see the number of divorcing people who blame an affair for the end of their marriage. Rather than seeing it as a symptom of a bad relationship, a spouse may consider it the cause of the break-up. Apparently, a number of people who want to end their marriage see infidelity as a clear way to go about it. While one might assume that it is easy to end a marriage, that's generally not the case. One person will want to continue, and the one who wants out has no "good enough" reason to divorce. An affair changes those dynamics—now there is good reason. The deceit that typically surrounds an affair invariably results in a lack of trust by the spouse, who labels the affair a betrayal.

If a potential client is a betrayed spouse, and reads or hears that I advise individuals with a financially distrustful spouse *not* to use mediation (see page 24), he may think, "If she had an affair and lied to me, of course, she'd lie about her finances." This is rarely true. During my seventeen-plus years' experience as a mediator, I'd estimate that one spouse in well over half of the couples has had an affair. An affair is common in the portrait of a divorcing couple, while actual financial dishonesty is not.

Mediation can be very effective even though your spouse is having an affair. In fact, situations that are emotionally explosive, that include feelings of rage and betrayal, have so much to lose in the adversarial world that these couples are much better off in mediation. The adversarial court system and the divorce lawyers can fan those angry flames. The faithful spouse has intense feelings of anger and hurt, and those strong emotions could propel a court action that would cost thousands of dollars, and yet a judge cannot resolve the issue of an affair. The mediator cannot resolve it either; however, he can help focus on what's important, as well as allow each side the opportunity to be heard. A courtroom is a place to resolve legal disputes; an affair is a personal issue. Someone may say, "Legally, isn't adultery a crime?" Yes, in many states it is, but they don't put people in jail for committing adultery.

4. LACK OF COMMUNICATION:

Sometimes I'm asked how a couple will be able to mediate if they don't speak to each other. I explain that they can communicate through the mediator. Keep in mind that the inability to talk to each other is common for a divorcing couple. People who barely speak to each other at the start of mediation will eventually start talking. Mediators are not magicians, but they have the skills to help people to communicate. (However, before you assume that mediation means reconciliation, let me point out that it doesn't.)

5. CHILD CUSTODY DISPUTES:

The other night I was at a dinner party when the man sitting next to me asked me what I did for a living. When I explained I was a divorce mediator, he responded, "I wish that I had used you three years ago when I needed you. My wife and I had a terrible custody battle over our two kids." When I asked him why he didn't use mediation, he replied, "Well, I know that mediation is for people who get along well. But we didn't. Not that the court helped us get along. Fact is, the judge and those others only made it worse. Things are really bad between us now."

His comments regarding who is appropriate for mediation are typical. Mediation has developed a reputation as a forum for couples who get along well. As I've said, there are very few divorcing couples who fit that description. Certainly, couples who get along well also do well in mediation, but it's definitely not a requirement.

Years ago, mediation proved itself within the field of disputed child custody battles—arguments in which there is strong unresolved anger, bitterness, and fear. It is the most difficult of conflicts. Early studies focused on the mediation of these disputes because research, common sense, and our own eyes showed us that the children affected by these traumatic custody battles suffered terrible emotional scars. In spite of parents spending thousands of dollars in what each believed was the best interests of a child, all parties suffered. Said one Massachusetts judge, "Custody battles are more difficult to hear than murder trials."

In just about every state, custody is an open door. The court always has jurisdiction over child custody, and a parent can always go to court to petition a change in custody if it is in the best interest of a child. Because of this, a parent who is dissatisfied with a court decision can bring a new court action, propelling both parents into court again. Mediation helps to resolve the issue of custody in a way that both parents can live with, so that neither feels the need to litigate further.

Studies show that the mediation of custody disputes works. In

1993 southern California mediator Nina R. Meierding analyzed the Ventura County Superior Court records of couples who reached a divorce settlement through a private mediator. The purpose of her survey was to measure long-term satisfaction and compliance to mediated agreements. She found that the survey dramatically illustrated the high level of satisfaction of divorcing couples who used private mediation.

The State of California mandated that every couple arguing custody use the services of a mediator to resolve their dispute. Today, that practice continues, and states throughout the country are following suit by considering legislation that requires all custody disputants to use a mediator. I predict that, eventually, the common practice will be to send all custody disputes to a mediator.

6. LEAVING THE MARITAL RESIDENCE DISPUTES:

For most couples about to divorce, that first step of separating is a difficult one. How does one spouse move out of the marital residence, whether it's a house, condominium, or apartment? In some cases, there is a specific problem. For example, a couple has made the decision that the wife will move out, but prior to leaving, she consults with her lawyer, and the lawyer advises her not to. Ostensibly, the lawyer does this to protect the client from later changing her mind and wanting use of the marital residence. She feels stuck, wanting to separate but not willing to go against the advice of her lawyer. In this all-too-common situation, the tension rises, and two people are forced to go on living together under conditions of great tension.

During an impending separation, practical money matters must be addressed. The spouse moving out typically needs money to rent an apartment or buy a house. People recognize that buying real estate is expensive. Renting a place is also expensive, since most landlords require the current month's rent as well as the last month's, and most places also require a security deposit. Mediation offers a way for couples to work through the difficult decision of who must leave, as well as other crucial questions: When? Should both leave? Who pays the moving expenses? Who pays the other expenses? It probably comes as no surprise, but it costs more money to run two households than one, yet there is not more money coming in. How, then, shall the couple allocate their resources? Separation comes with myriad other questions: Who will continue to pay joint debt? Who is responsible for the mortgage or the rent? Should the address on legal forms be changed? What will it mean if the address does change? Mediators can help generate answers to these questions. Many assume that separation is a simple process, but there are issues, including legal ones, that must be addressed and resolved. A mediator can help people reach good decisions, as well as lay a foundation for future decision making.

Some couples think that if they use a mediator to work out the details of a separation, it means that they must proceed to a divorce settlement. For those who want a separation but do not see divorce as their final goal, a decision to separate does not necessarily mean a decision to divorce. A mediator can provide help with the terms of the separation.

7. LAWYERS ALREADY HIRED:

I do a fair amount of public speaking about divorce mediation, and a frequent comment is "My wife and I already have lawyers, so I guess it's too late for us to use a mediator." The often surprising answer is that's not true. Even if one or both of you have hired a lawyer, it's still not too late to use mediation. Though the mediator cannot give you back the money you've spent on legal fees, your future costs will be dramatically reduced. If you want an idea of how much money you'll save if you use a mediator, ask several divorcing people who used attorneys how much they spent, and then subtract mediation fees. The amount may shock you.

Also ask how long it was from the day a lawyer was hired to the date of divorce. Many people assume that if more than two months have passed since they hired their lawyers, they are al-most done with the divorce process and it's too late to use a me-diator. It's rarely too late, even if a fair amount of time has passed. However, if you are looking for the support of your lawyer for mediation, chances are, you may not get it. Not that all lawyers oppose mediation; indeed, a growing number do support it, but remember, for most lawyers, mediation means less earnings. It would be a little strange if they all were enthusi-astic about earning less.

8. ALREADY DIVORCED:

Arguments that arise after the divorce is final are called post-divorce disputes. For couples who use attorneys to reach a divorce settlement, post-divorce disputes are not unusual. Me-diators who do post-divorce work are generally not in session with prior mediation clients; more likely, their clients used at-torneys or wrote a divorce settlement on their own, and they now turn to a mediator to solve a new dispute.

Mediation clients are much less likely to need post-divorce help in reaching an agreement. Fewer than 1 percent of my clients do. However, some couples do return to mediation to re-solve an issue. When disputes occur, they tend to occur among ex-spouses who have minor children and financial ties.

The usual course of meetings for post-divorce mediation de-pends on whether or not the couple used a mediator to reach their divorce settlement. If they did use mediation, I meet them together. I use a different approach with clients who did not use mediation, meeting them jointly for part of the session, and then separately.

Post-divorce negotiation is often more difficult than negotia-tions before the divorce. During a marriage, both spouses may be motivated to be reasonable in order to work things out, but that's not true after divorce, when neither person seems highly motivated to be reasonable. Generally the more specific the agreement clients work out at the time of the divorce, the fewer arguments erupt at a later date.

9. SUBSTANCE ABUSE:

One day a psychologist friend of mine, Donna, called me. "I was going to refer a couple to you who requested the name of a good mediator, but I wondered if they could use mediation," she said.

"Why is that?" I asked.

"Well, the wife has an alcohol abuse problem, and my understanding is that one needs to be clear-headed in mediation."

"Do you see her while she's drunk?" I asked.

"Of course not," Donna responded. "We schedule sessions during the morning, and she's fine then."

"Then," I said, "we could schedule mediation sessions during the morning or any other time when she's fine. By 'fine,' you mean not drunk or drinking, right?"

"Yes," Donna replied, "that she is not under the influence. Somehow it never occurred to me that if she could do therapy, she could do mediation."

Couples in mediation reflect couples in our society. Because of the prevalence of alcohol and drug abuse in our culture, and because clients are representatives of the culture we live in, many couples who use mediation have a problem with alcohol or drugs. In order to mediate with an individual who is a substance abuser, whether alcohol or another kind of a drug, he or she must be sober/clean during the mediation sessions. Mediation is also possible when the person is in treatment. Mediation is *not* possible except under these conditions (see page 25).

Indeed, in certain cases, mediation can provide an ideal forum for those couples affected by alcohol or drug abuse. If there are children involved, during the mediation, the parents can take alcohol and/or drug abuse into consideration and are able to be open about their drinking without fear of legal repercussions. The mediation room is not a court of law, and there is no public record. Rather, it allows an honest airing of concerns and the opportunity to explore solutions. In a public courtroom, people who are accused of such abuses will typically deny the seriousness and extent of the use. During mediation, the mediator works with the client to assure child safety, rather than to focus on blame.

•   •   •

None of these problems I've just discussed are reasons not to use mediation, particularly if the mediator has significant expertise in the areas that must be addressed. However, there are a few instances when I feel that mediation usually is not appropriate. These are:

1. Financial dishonesty
2. Severe substance abuse
3. Untreated serious mental illness
4. Domestic violence

1. FINANCIAL DISHONESTY:
Considered inappropriate for mediation are financially dishonest people, men and women who fit the following specific description: They lie about money to their spouses; they will continue to lie during the mediation sessions; their spouses do not know the true financial situation; and most important, the lie(s) is/are significant. All factors must be present to rule someone out of mediation. For example, if your husband is a civil servant and says that he has no other income, and yet you live in an expensive, mortgage-free house in the most exclusive section of town, this may be an example of a significant lie. Warning bells should ring. (Actually, they should have rung years ago!)

If you think your spouse has lied about finances, you must decide whether the lies are significant enough to make the mediation process inappropriate. I once encountered a man who said he wanted to use mediation, but he didn't think he could because his wife was dishonest about finances. I asked what he meant. "Well, just last week she told me that she hadn't bought anything new," he said, "and yet today I found a receipt for a new blouse on her bureau." The question that he had to answer was whether or not the wife's lie about the purchase of a blouse was significant in terms of its implications for the mediation process. Because she had lied about the blouse, would she lie about some significant asset? Was she lying because she had no access to her own money? Or was it an accepted pattern in the marriage for dealing with clothes purchases by the wife? Does her purchase and subsequent lie about the blouse mean that she will withhold important financial information? This is something he must decide, but in my experience, such a situation would not preclude mediation.

2. SEVERE SUBSTANCE ABUSE:

As I said earlier, mediation is possibly only if the abuser can be sober/clean during the mediation sessions or is in treatment. If your spouse is actively drinking or doing drugs and cannot attend a session when clean/sober, mediation is inappropriate. It is impossible to mediate when someone is under the influence of alcohol or drugs.

3. UNTREATED SERIOUS MENTAL ILLNESS:

If either spouse is mentally ill and is unable to take part meaningfully in the mediation process, that couple is not appropriate for mediation. Only if that person can function competently while on prescription drugs would he or she be able to take part. For instance, a man once called to say, "My wife has a diagnosis of schizophrenia, and she's not taking her medicine." I don't let myself be influenced by a mediating client, so we set up a free introductory session. Sure enough, during our session, she appeared unable to function because she said she was hearing voices. I concluded that the couple was not appropriate for mediation.

In only one of my cases did one spouse consider the other too mentally ill to take part in mediation. A woman said her husband was "crazy." She told him one night that she was leaving him and didn't like the way he was acting—sometimes upset and angry, other times hurt and sad. However, when they came to the mediation table, he seemed like every other client. What she saw as mental illness may simply have been stress over the sudden knowledge of the divorce. Sometimes, people in the midst of a divorce may not see their spouses as clearly as a professional can, and they may overreact to behavior that doesn't seem normal.

4. DOMESTIC VIOLENCE:

Situations of domestic violence create the most difficult dilemma as to whether or not to mediate. This subject is by far the most hotly debated topic within the field of mediation. In the United States, the extent and pervasiveness of domestic violence has only recently come to our attention. For many, the issue was tragically brought to the forefront with the murder of Nicole Brown Simpson. The famous O. J. Simpson, who some label a chronic wife-abuser, was on trial for his life, defended by a team of high-priced lawyers. Would O. J. and Nicole have been appropriate candidates for mediation? What about those abusers who are not alleged to be or tried as murderers?

The term *domestic violence* is generally defined as the use of physical force, or the threat of such force, to gain control over a current or former spouse or lover. The acts of domestic violence include pushing, slapping, hitting, choking, shoving, using a weapon, physically restraining, or the threat of any of these.

Domestic violence is unlike other types of violence in that there is frequently a pattern, called the cycle of violence. We know that the rate of abuse increases at certain times. One of these times is when the woman is pregnant and most vulnerable to her mate while his jealousy of the coming baby intensifies. Another event that can trigger abuse is when the wife separates from her husband. This act exacerbates his feelings of abandonment and the corresponding attack on his self-esteem.

In all situations of domestic violence, the differences in power between spouses is extremely unbalanced. The perpetrator has all the power. The victim has virtually none, and most of the time, she is too terrified of her husband to use what little power she does have. Were she in mediation, she would not be able to state her settlement interests because of the fear that, after the session, he would beat her simply for stating her wants. Traditional divorce mediation, with both spouses in the same room, cannot work with couples who are in the classic male battering cycle of violence. Many courts recognize this and have instituted rules prohibiting mediation when domestic violence is evident. You absolutely cannot mediate the violence, which means the mediator cannot condone the trade-off of "I'll give you what you want if you don't beat me." Most experts in the field advise the victim never to mediate if abuse has been or is currently a factor.

SCREENING FOR DOMESTIC VIOLENCE

Two Schools of Thought

If the courts do not forbid it, the issue of whether private divorce mediators should work with clients of domestic violence is controversial. A number of mediators believe that a mediator should *not* work with a victim of domestic violence under any circumstances. However, since a mediator cannot determine if someone is a victim or a perpetrator by merely looking at him or her, this group believes that a mediator must screen potential clients in order to determine if domestic violence exists or existed. If the screening indicates violence in the relationship (currently or in the past), the mediator will decline to work with the couple. Screening typically involves a written test given separately to each spouse.

Other mediators do not agree. These mediators do not screen and, in fact, regard screening as biased (against the alleged perpetrator). They believe that a good mediator will learn during the session if there is an issue of domestic violence. The theory here is that if there is domestic violence, which interferes with the mediation process, it will surface, and then the mediator can treat the issue as an instance of power imbalance (which a good mediator should be able to address).

Typically, a mediator who screens does so with every client, and the screening is administered separately to each one. The mediator does not simply ask, "Have you ever been beaten?" Nor can the mediator ask, "Has there been domestic violence?" because study after study has shown that women answer no to both questions. No one wants to be identified as a victim.

If you are a victim of abuse, please understand that many mediators will screen you out of the process. If you are determined to use mediation, there are competent mediators who can work with you, but you must proceed with caution. It is imperative that your mediator have the following qualifications: (1) understand the cycle of violence; (2) have received training to deal with the victim and the perpetrator of domestic violence; (3) understand all of the safety issues; (4) have a referral network with shelter advocates; (5) know the available legal action; and (6) have five or more years' experience as a mediator, at least some with clients where there has been domestic violence. However, it will be up to you to know and follow all safety precautions.

Prior to mediation, you should consult with a woman's advocate (an expert in the field of domestic violence) as well as someone who can advise you as to how appropriate mediation is to your specific situation. The violence must be over, and you absolutely must not be in physical danger from your husband, nor fear him. Finally, you may want to obtain or keep in place a legal restraining order. You must choose an experienced mediator who knows and follows safety rules (one typical rule is that spouses must leave the office separately with approximately twenty minutes in between each leave-taking, so that the perpetrator cannot follow the victim), and you must admit any abuse to the mediator.

To repeat, it is crucial that you choose a mediator who is knowledgeable in the field of domestic violence. Do not hesitate to question potential mediators as to whether they can and are willing to mediate if domestic violence is present. Ask for their comments. When I mediate with couples who are in this situation, I caucus with each individual, which means meeting separately with each client. Often I must caucus because there is a legal restraining order that prohibits the perpetrator from being near the victim. However, in situations of domestic violence, it is common to caucus whether or not there is a restraining order in effect. Let me add, however, that I have seen a number of divorcing couples where the woman's attorney advised the client to obtain a restraining order in order to gain legal leverage when there was no abuse nor any fear of abuse. This misuse of a restraining order is a travesty of justice and creates almost as much difficulty for the mediator as the issue of domestic violence, because there is also a victim, the unfairly accused husband. Mediation is a field with very few formal rules, so not all mediators may caucus with every case of domestic violence. As a client, you need to decide what you want and need. As always, the more you know about what your choices are, the better your chance of reaching your goal.

If the violence has ended, mediation can work if all of these factors are in place, but *it cannot work* if all are not present. Remember, there is no excuse for hitting someone. It is the perpetrator who has destroyed the chance of mediation, not the victim.

There are cases where violence has occurred in the past, but the present situation is stable. If this is your situation, mediation may be appropriate. For example, Stan and June presented a stable current situation with a past incident of domestic violence and no current fear by the victim. They had been married for twenty-six years and separated for four months. Their discussion revealed that at age seventeen, June discovered that she was pregnant, and married her nineteen-year-old boyfriend,

Stan. Stan quit college and got a full-time job (although in later years he took college classes during the evenings). Both sets of parents were angry and called daily to give the "kids" a piece of their mind. June was sick all of the time, not just in the morning. One evening at dinner, June was angry over what she considered a useless and frivolous purchase Stan had made. To this day, neither remembers what the item was, but both recall the situation. June made a nasty insult to Stan, who quickly got up from the kitchen table, tore his new shirt on the table edge, yelled back at her, and pushed her against the wall. That night June told Stan she'd leave him if he ever pushed her or did anything like that again. He swore he wouldn't, and a significant issue is that he has never hit her nor used threatening behavior since that time. When they began mediation, June was not afraid of Stan, nor did she fear him during the mediation process. Though this couple did have an episode of domestic violence in their past, they were indeed appropriate candidates for mediation.

You Feel Afraid

I place a subgroup of people into the category of domestic violence even though there has been no history of violence. In these situations, the wife is afraid and feels threatened by her spouse, although her husband has never hit her. She is not able to stand up for herself for fear that she will be physically assaulted for the comments she makes during mediation. Do not ignore your feelings. Remember, domestic violence rates increase significantly at times of separation. A potential abuser may resort to violence when his partner walks out the door. If you are afraid that your spouse will hit you and that you will not be able to stand up for yourself and ask for what you want, mediation is not for you.

If you want to use mediation but are married to someone for whom it is not appropriate, I sympathize, but I assure you that the process will not work if your spouse is financially dishonest, is a serious substance abuser, or is seriously mentally ill. In the instance of domestic abuse it will not work unless you have a mediator with a great deal of expertise in this area, and since this is rare, my advice is not to use mediation unless you are highly motivated, understand all the precautions and risks, and know that you are employing a mediator with the expertise to handle this most difficult of situations.

3

Getting Your Spouse to Use Mediation

At least once a day—more often three or four times—an urgent-sounding caller asks this question: "I want to use mediation and not get divorce lawyers involved. What can I say so that my spouse will agree to see a mediator?"

"It's not easy," I reply, "but I can certainly give you some ideas." For many divorcing men and women, the problem is not so much about a basic difference concerning how to resolve conflict. Rather, it's that during divorce, a spouse is distrustful of any idea that emanates from the other. The distrust is created in two ways. First, the societal attitude encircling divorce holds that the end of a marriage should mean anger and bitterness (when, in fact, some couples are looking for a civilized approach). The adversarial system has created a world whereby if one spouse says "black" the other is sure to answer "white," and on and on it goes. Where once there was a way for this couple to make joint decisions, the means for suggestions, discussion, and agreements have eroded. This makes taking that first step toward the mediator's office a very difficult one.

The second way in which distrust is created between divorcing spouses is that one spouse changes—too often manifested by having an affair. The human response to infidelity is hurt and anger, often translating into revenge. The faithful spouse's feeling of betrayal is intense. Though the affair is often a symptom of the marital problems, it is treated as a cause, a reason for the break-up.

Change may also be exhibited by an individual's emotional midlife crisis, or becoming sober, or embarking on a new career. To the spouse who has not changed so dramatically, it feels like a betrayal. During one session with my clients, Peter and Marie, married twenty-one years, he suddenly turned to his wife and, with bitter resentment, accused her, "Listen to the way you're talking—you've changed since I first met you." Too often, we do not allow our spouse to change; we expect him or her to stay the same. But, of course, change is inevitable. We all change, though many relationships seek to deny or prevent a spouse from doing so.

In the typical situation, one that rings true for more than 95 percent of the couples I see, either the husband or wife is reluctant or, more accurately, resistant to the divorce. When someone does not want a divorce, it only stands to reason that the individual may very well reject a process that leads to divorce, no matter how civilized and cost-effective it is.

Couples with the best chance of getting into mediation with the least amount of pain are those in which both spouses want the divorce and neither blames the other. In fact, prior to the divorce, they are typically considered the perfect couple. These exceptional divorcing couples mutually accept the termination of their relationship and many even intend to remain friends. Most people would expect, and it is generally true, that these couples used marriage counseling to try and save their marriage. What is less expected but is just as true is that they have reached an understanding that each needs to separate in order to be able to sustain individual growth and well-being. This man and woman acknowledge the sadness which pervades the end of a relationship, and though many divorcing couples acknowledge this feeling, what makes this couple unique is that neither partner is stuck in the anger stage of the divorce cycle. The anger is there, of course, along with other conflicting emotions, it is just not all-consuming.

Those friendly divorces do not emphasize the hateful attitude that typifies the usual demeanor of those about to end a marriage. The angry behavior so often exhibited is not evident; indeed, friends and relatives, neighbors and co-workers are all shocked that this couple is on the road to divorce.

Typically, this seemingly perfect couple receives very little support from the people in their lives in their decision to divorce. In fact, the couple may be each other's best support person, as only the spouse truly understands the paradox that although they care for each other and are compatible, each believes that divorce is the best route. Even the divorce professionals who come in contact with this couple may find that the end of this relationship is harder to accept than most.

In our society, we accept divorce only as a last resort for situations in which a man and woman cannot live together without causing themselves or their children an unconscionable existence—where physical beatings, alcohol or drug abuse, cheating, and the like occur—and even then, we wonder if there isn't another solution. We have come to our modern-day acceptance of divorce reluctantly. When we read of violence permeating the lives of a husband and wife, when we personally visit a couple whose house resonates with constant yelling and disparaging remarks, when a woman or a man continues to drink, we will accept the termination of the marriage. But when a married couple are civil to each other and appear to care for each other, society questions and even rejects the termination of that relationship.

Why do people become upset upon hearing that a seemingly perfect couple is considering divorce? Virtually all married people consider divorce, if only for a fleeting moment. They may wonder—if only for a second—if they should continue in their marriage or if divorce wouldn't free them to experience something else. And the divorce of the seemingly perfect couple exacerbates that momentary vision of something else. For if that couple chooses divorce, what of those who are not perfect? Shouldn't they divorce as well? The divorce of the "perfect couple" threatens those who choose to continue in their marriages.

Married people are not alone in feeling threatened by the divorce of the perfect couple. It also threatens those who are not married but hope to be one day. Single people look to the seemingly perfect couple as the ideal embodiment of marital life. Over the years, studies have conclusively shown that men and women alike believe in marriage. They invest heavily in being able to predict which couples will make it and who then become role models for married life. If that kind of couple divorces, people may question whether anyone can make a marriage work.

In one area, though, the couple does receive support. Their decision to use mediation meets with approval from friends and family. Secretly, however, these friends and family confide the hope that mediation will end in reconciliation. Yet, the couple has decided upon a specific future—one which does not include the other.

As a mediator, I have a number of seemingly perfect couples among my clients. However, you can rightly assume that most couples do not fit this profile. In the majority of the couples I see, one spouse does not want the marriage to end and holds the other spouse responsible for initiating the break-up. In these situations, the spouse who calls me must deal with the first step: how to get his or her spouse to use mediation.

The best way to get your spouse to consider mediation is to first provide him or her with information about the process. Since the mediator has had the opportunity to speak with the calling spouse, the information packet was designed to explain the benefits of mediation to the spouse who is uninformed or ambivalent. I have included a sample packet at the end of the book (see appendix C, page 121). Once he or she is aware of it, the benefits of mediation are likely to appeal. Often, a caller wants me to call his or her spouse to convince that individual to attend a mediation session. This is not something I can do. A mediator cannot make an unsolicited call.

I receive many calls from individuals who are still living with their spouses. In these cases, even though one spouse doesn't want the divorce and there is a lot of blame, the situation makes it easier to deliver the information packet as well as to describe the advantages of mediation. Though a period of time spent living together in anticipation of divorce is a stressful time of life, the fact that you are still living together may make it easier to share information.

If the couple have already separated and are living apart, I try to help the caller find an appropriate way to get the information to the spouse. In some relatively calm situations, he or she will simply be able to send it, the spouse will read it and wish to cooperate in mediation. However, for many people, it won't be that easy. Such a caller is aware that the spouse is too angry and resentful to read any material; therefore, the caller needs to figure out another way to get him or her to read the information.

If you think your spouse may be resistant to information that comes from you, the best way is to find someone whom your spouse knows who has actually used mediation. If the person happens to be a close friend, his or her approval will carry a lot of weight. However, even if it isn't a friend and is instead a neighbor or an acquaintance, do not underestimate the importance of a personal recommendation. If someone is considering mediation but is wary of embarking on an unknown process, such words are invaluable. When you first consider mediation, mention this to a number of people. You may get some help.

If you don't know anyone who has personally used a mediator, another option is to find someone who is still on speaking terms with both of you and who you think may be supportive of mediation. Since that person might never have heard about mediation, you will need to supply details, and an information packet is a good way to start. The use of a mutual friend or a relative is an excellent way to get your spouse to consider mediation. However, I find that less than half of my clients have such a person in their lives.

There is just one person that you cannot use—your minor child. In the adversarial system, both parties are strongly—and rightly—advised to keep the child out of it, to protect the child from the two parents. Causing such harm is not a by-product of the mediation process. Instead, studies of children whose parents are in mediation have consistently shown that these children have a significantly better adjustment to divorce. Children benefit enormously when their parents use mediation. Let me be clear: I am *not* recommending that a parent attempt to get the child on his or her side or to use the child against the other parent.

However, in trying to obtain the cooperation of your spouse to try mediation, the assistance of an *adult* child is invaluable. It works best if the child is at least beyond high school age. But there are no hard and fast rules. The emotional maturity of people differs, and the emphasis on adult child is *adult*. Remember, you need to be clear that the only help you are asking from your child is getting your spouse to consider mediation.

A good number of the divorcing couples I see have been married for a long time, thirty to forty years. For these men and women in their fifties and sixties, it is not uncommon that the person who brought up the idea of a mediator was their adult child. I am always moved when parents confide in me that it was their child who first made the suggestion. Typically, these clients had not heard of mediation until their son or daughter suggested it. These parents trust that their child has their best interests at heart.

The callers who are the most upset are those whose spouses have consulted with a lawyer. Such situations often require creative methods for getting their spouses to use mediation. Recently, when I spoke to a caller, Gary, his voice reflected how upset he was. Anxiously, he explained, "My wife hired a divorce lawyer, and she had me served with a summons while I was at work. Would you believe that a sheriff came to my office and actually served me with a summons in front of everyone? I felt like a criminal, which, I'm sure, is exactly what she wanted. She succeeded in humiliating me.

"I went to talk to a lawyer," he continued, "to reply to that summons, and he advised me to retaliate. He said that I could get her. Of course, then he asked for his $10,000 retainer! Now, I'm not stupid. I know this will just turn into a costly war. The only ones who will win are the divorce lawyers. I don't want to spend money for that."

I asked what he would like to do. "I want to use a mediator," he replied. "But I just don't know how to get her to come."

In divorce, revenge may be sweet, but as Gary pointed out, it is also costly. He was sophisticated enough to realize that a retainer is only the upfront money. His lawyer described legal action that would use up that money in no time, so that Gary's legal fees would be substantially higher as the adversarial course escalated.

Not long after, a woman named Judy called. She said that she had seen a canceled check from her and her husband's joint checking account that her husband had written to his lawyer, for $7,500. On the morning of her call to me, her husband told her he would be writing yet another check to his lawyer. Judy was upset. "He's forcing me to hire a lawyer, but I really don't want to spend all our savings on lawyers," she said. "We are not wealthy people. I know that there has to be another way." When I asked her how I could help, she replied, "I want us to use a mediator, but I don't know how to go about getting my husband to meet with you."

I suggested to both Gary and Judy that they write a letter to their spouses and enclose the mediation packet I would send them. I told them that in their letters they should outline their concerns and suggest that the couple see a mediator in order to reach a fair divorce settlement. I told them to be sure to say that they could call the mediator first and to suggest that the spouse also seek the names of additional mediators. I explained that they both could come in for a free introductory session. And above all, I said, remember to be polite and listen to your spouse's concerns.

Shortly after my conversation with Gary, he and his wife scheduled a mediation session and successfully reached a divorce settlement, spending $1,740 on mediation fees, which included their divorce agreement, and without incurring any additional legal fees. Judy and her husband also used mediation. Their total mediation cost was $2,110, which also included the cost of their divorce agreement. Judy had an additional legal bill of $345 for an attorney she consulted. Her husband had already spent $12,500 on his attorney fees.

If writing to your spouse doesn't work, another way is to ask him or her to read a book or article about the subject. Sending the book or article is a lot more effective than simply providing the name or title, because the latter option requires your spouse to do extra work—to go to a library or to a bookstore. It makes sense for you to take the extra step.

A couple, Robert and Julie, once had a terrible argument in my office after she found out that he had never read my first book before sending it to her and suggesting she read it, which she did. Julie complained that her husband had once again done less work than she—an old, sore issue with Julie. She felt that Robert went through the motions of working on their relationship, but he didn't do the actual work (here represented by reading the book), while she carried the burden. They continued in mediation, but it caused a lot of unnecessary turmoil. It is always helpful to have written material to share with your spouse. Good written information helps people to make good choices. A reminder—and an important one—first read any book or other material that you send to your spouse. (See the resource list on page 194 for a list of helpful books.)

Let me add one absolute: *Do not, under any conditions, send material that in any way insults or disparages your spouse or his or her behavior.* A woman named Susan once called and told me that she had sent her husband an article about men who run off with their secretaries; her husband had an affair with his secretary and was now living with her. According to Susan, the article described the terrible consequences for that man's wife and children and, as far as I could surmise, the later anguish and regret of the errant husband. "Now," Susan said, "I want to send information about mediation to my husband, but he told me that he's so angry with me that he will return unread anything I send him. He's already sent back something important I sent him. He's really mad, which is so ridiculous. I'm the one who should be mad. He left me."

Susan is an example of a spouse who is either unable or unwilling to accept the consequences of her actions and has little insight into her interactions with her spouse. Such lack of insight makes it difficult for couples to reach an initial agreement to use mediation.

A number of callers are concerned that their spouses will automatically discard or ignore the material. If this applies to your case, try to think of another way to get your spouse to read the information. Keep in mind that you are the expert on your spouse. As you consider your approach, keep that knowledge foremost.

In many communities, various agencies (community divorce and resource centers, adult education seminars, lawyer and/or counseling groups) offer public lectures on separation and divorce, which can be a great way to introduce your spouse to mediation. However, be certain to give your spouse the option of going to the event separately from you, or offer to refrain from going yourself so that he or she can go alone. You might say something like, "There is a lecture on mediation next Wednesday evening. I'd like us to consider mediation, and I want to know if you'd go to the lecture to find out more about it. I'd be glad to let you decide whether we both go, and if so, if we sit together, or if you prefer that I don't go." And then, most important of all, listen to your spouse's response. Do not argue. If necessary, explain and offer to explain some more. And always, in any discussion with your spouse, keep mud-slinging comments out of it.

As I've said, our office, like those of many other mediators, offers a free introductory session because a significant number of people want more information about the mediation process, as well as about the mediator, in order to make an informed decision. They are understandably concerned about venturing forward without enough facts to feel comfortable. An introductory session provides an important opportunity to meet the mediator, to hear about the mediation process, and to ask questions. Take advantage of this opportunity. If the mediator doesn't offer a free introductory session, nothing prohibits you from asking for one and, in fact, I suggest that you do. I have had clients who are so anxious to begin the process that they ask if they can skip the introductory session. My answer is that not only is it free, it is important. It is a rare couple who attends an introductory session and does not decide to use mediation. Once they hear what a common sense approach it is, they invariably choose the process. Though I don't keep actual statistics on this, I would estimate that not more than a half-dozen couples a year, out of more than three hundred couples who come to an introductory session each year, fail to mediate. So, while you are describing the mediation process to your spouse, do not forget to tell him or her about the free introductory session.

In one situation, getting mediation information to a spouse does present a serious problem—when there is a restraining order on one or both of the spouses that prohibits one from sending mail to the other. In the vast majority of situations, it is the woman who has obtained a restraining order on the man. (It is rare for me to see husbands getting restraining orders on their wives, though it does occur.) Whichever the case, in a typical order, *neither* can send mail to the other. My advice is that if a restraining order that prohibits sending material is present *do not defy the order*, even if you consider your intentions good. Instead, you must find an intermediary to deliver the information, or apply to the court for a waiver of the order in order to allow you to send it or have your lawyer send it to your spouse's lawyer.

At the end of one mediation, a client, Richard, wanted to tell me how he and his wife had decided to use a mediator. He arrived home one evening, listened to his answering machine, and heard a friend recommend a movie to him. Richard said the message sounded like, "Go see *Disclosure*—you'll appreciate it." Sure enough, Richard went to see the movie, and he was so impressed that the characters portrayed by Demi Moore and Michael Douglas chose to use a mediator that he suggested mediation to his wife. She considered it and agreed. Weeks later he saw his friend and thanked him for the suggestion. *Disclosure?* his friend responded in a surprised voice. "You know that's not my type of movie. I said, *Death Wish!*"

• • •

Consider these suggestions and choose the ones that you think will work best with your spouse. After all, divorce professionals are just experts in their fields, not experts on your wife or husband. You know your spouse best, even if she or he may be temporarily acting in a way that is out of character. Be positive. Do not give up before you try. You have nothing to lose and everything to gain if your spouse will mediate.

4

Assessing Your Needs:
What Do You Want
from a Mediator?

Once you begin looking for a mediator, you'll find out that not only do we come in all shapes and sizes, our professional backgrounds differ as well. Virtually all other individuals within the same profession have similar backgrounds. For example, all lawyers have graduated from law school; all doctors have graduated from medical school; all accountants have graduated with a degree in accounting. The story is different with mediators; there is no common background. Many mediators do take a forty-hour divorce mediation course, but certainly not all do, and most likely not even a majority. Some mediators did attend law school, others studied social work, and still others attended business school; however, a significant number have no graduate degree, and some never went to college at all. However, rather than focusing first on the qualifications of the mediator, look at yourself. What are *your* needs in a divorce mediator?

In the pages that follow, I list the characteristics that a good mediator should possess and that a divorcing man or woman may need. Read through it and get a general feel for the types of issues. Then do a second review, this time arranging your priorities. On the third review, focus on your specific needs—generally, the top three requirements for your situation. If your circumstances are complicated, you might look for a mediator who meets four or five of your needs. Do not assume that you must focus on every need—that would be both daunting and unnecessary. Instead, prioritize.

Your Situation	*Qualifications of the Mediator*
1. Have children:	Background in child development
	Knowledge of latest research on parenting arrangements
	Familiar with local court practices regarding custody plans that a court will approve
	Familiar with legal definition of custody
a. Financial concerns/ support guidelines:	Understanding of your state child custody laws
	Expertise in:
	• Child dependency tax rules
	• Head of household tax rules
	• Household budgeting
	• Rules for custodial accounts
b. Insurance:	Applicable state and federal laws pertaining to medical and/or dental insurance coverage for children
2. Own a house:	Expertise in:
a. May want joint ownership:	• Real estate transactions
b. May want to sell:	• Federal and state capital gains taxes
c. May want a buy-out:	• Title and deed transfers
	• Mortgage qualifications and refinancing

Your Situation	*Qualifications of the Mediator*
	• Buy-out tax consequences, including the IRS tax code, Incident to Divorce Rule
d. Mortgage greater than house value:	Expertise in: • Mortgage financing • Sale in lieu of foreclosure • Liability exposure
e. May want to buy:	Expertise in: • Mortgage qualifications and financing • Real estate market • Fanny Mae requirements
3. Pensions and retirement plans:	Expertise in: • Pension plans • Retirement plans • Transfers of pensions and retirement plans • Employee Retirement Income Security Act (ERISA) • Qualified Domestic Relations Orders • Federal and state tax consequences • Withdrawal rules and penalties • Incident to Divorce Rule

4. An apartment:
  a. Live in an apartment:
  b. Will move into an apartment:
	Expertise in:
	• State laws regarding rental deductions

Your Situation	*Qualifications of the Mediator*
5. Medical and dental insurance coverage:	Expertise in: • Applicable laws concerning coverage of an ex-spouse • State health and dental insurance statutes • Federal COBRA laws (Consolidated Omnibus Budget Reduction Act) • QUAMCSO (Qualified Medical Child Support Orders) • ERISA
6. Investment accounts, stocks, bonds, and mutual funds:	Understanding of: • Types of financial investments • Taxable capital gains and losses • Federal and state taxes • Investment "basis" and computations
7. Credit card debt:	Understanding of: • Credit laws • Credit card account transfers • Joint and individual liability
8. Future college payments:	Understanding of: • Financial Aid Forms (FAF) • Children's custodial accounts • Estimated college expenses • Parental needs/ contributions

Your Situation	*Qualifications of the Mediator*
9. Self-employed: a. Sole-proprietor:	Understanding of: • Schedule C of federal 1040 tax return • Ordinary/unusual business expenses • Business valuation
b. If incorporated:	• C Corporation rules • Subchapter S rules • Articles of Incorporation • Bylaws • Financial statements • Business valuation
10. Professional license:	Understanding of: • Applicable state laws • Local court practices • Valuations
11. Realty trusts and other trusts:	Understanding of: • Interest under a trust document • Asset interpretation (for divorce purposes) • General understanding of trusts
12. Over age 55:	Expertise in: • Primary residence • Tax exclusion for capital gains tax • Pension and retirement accounts • Withdrawal rules and penalties • Social Security rules

Your Situation	Qualifications of the Mediator
13. Lack of communication between spouses:	Psychological skills, such as reframing Couples counseling techniques
14. Not enough money to go around:	Understanding of: • Budgeting issues • Expense/income spreadsheets • Power dynamics • Underlying issues behind many arguments
15. Support payments (alimony):	Understanding of: • Alimony advantages/disadvantages • Spousal support vs. alimony • Federal and state tax consequences of alimony for payer and recipient
16. Alcohol/drug abuse:	Expertise in: • Substance abuse theory • Experience with this population • Drug/alcohol history taking • Psychological techniques in dealing with abuser
17. Domestic violence:	Understanding of: • Cycle of violence • Safety measures for clients and mediator • Local support references and network • Legal action available, especially restraining orders

Your Situation	*Qualifications of the Mediator*
18. Refusal to pay child support:	Knowledge of: • Applicable state law concerning child support payments • Court practices in your area • Wage assignments • Referral attorney network
19. Unusual parenting arrangements/division of assets:	Knowledge of: • Specific divorce court judges and decisions • Court practices in your area
20. Minimal funds (little or no assets to pay for mediation services):	Mediator offers: • Sliding scale based on financial situation • Negotiated payments for services • No retainer (money upfront) • Payment plan
21. A high-conflict couple/very argumentative	Primary profession as a mediator Experienced; five years full-time experience.

There is a considerable amount of information in these twenty-one situations. Let's look at each of these needs in more detail.

1. HAVE CHILDREN

Every state requires that a divorcing couple make custody arrangements for the children. A mediator will help you arrange a good parenting plan and can assist you with several aspects of custody decisions, from legal custody, which concerns who makes the major decisions concerning a child, and physical custody, which is the location where the child lives from day to day. The two basic physical custody arrangements involve a child living at one primary residence and spending time at another home (which courts often refer to as visitation), or joint physical custody, in which each parent has the child residing with him or her a good deal of time. Note that joint physical custody does not necessarily mean 50 percent of the time. A mediator can help parents look at the child's best interests, rather than at an arbitrary mathematical division of time.

There are many highly regarded studies concerning good parenting arrangements, and a mediator who is up on the latest research should prove invaluable. Even if they are not arguing over custody, many couples have questions concerning age-appropriate behavior, and a background in child development is helpful. For example, my clients Alan and Julie were considering whether it made sense to alternate one week on and one week off with their three-year-old son. Alan asked if there was any information I could provide regarding their child. I pointed out that it might be a good arrangement for the parents, which was important, but that a three-year-old will most likely have a hard time developmentally if he has a parent drop out of sight for an entire week. Some contact during that week with the non-residential parent would be beneficial for that toddler. The parents read two books I recommended, found another on their own, and talked to friends who had joint physical custody, and we later had further discussions on the matter. They jointly decided on a slightly different schedule, which called for the non-custodial parent to spend every Wednesday after school to an hour before bedtime with the boy. They also wanted to build in a review after three months to see if they needed to see their son more than once a week. A lot of factors figure into parenting arrangements, the ability of the child to handle transition not being the least. Many of the best custody schedules are not commonly known, even for the best of parents, which is why it is helpful to find a mediator who has a strong understanding of good parenting arrangements. Two uncommon schedules are (1) three overnights with one parent and four with the other, (2) primary residence with one parent and three out of four weekends with the other.

With children come a host of financial considerations. In response to federal mandates, every state has developed guidelines that decree the amount of child support that must be paid. Your mediator should be able to work out the guidelines with you and to provide you with that figure. You'll also need someone who can walk you through the likely issues that face ex-spouses in the future, so that the mediator can alert you to make those agreements now. For example, will child support change in the future? Will there be support when a child goes to college? If so, will support end or be adjusted? If one party makes a lot more money, will it affect the amount of child support? What if one loses a job? If you have no provision for these events, you will end up in a courtroom, with each of you paying thousands of dollars to a lawyer to confront these issues. I've seen hundreds of nonmediated cases where a man lost his job, and each parent was forced to go out and hire a lawyer (during a time when there was no money coming in) in order to adjust their child support payments. In mediation, couples will either write a renegotiation clause or actually decide what will happen. Since studies show that negotiations between ex-spouses become more difficult as times goes on, it makes sense for clients to make actual decisions or formulate guidelines concerning future adjustments. I think the reason this works best is because there's actually a strong bond between the couple at the time of divorce; the bond lessens over time, and ex-spouses become less attached.

Along with the financial child support issues, your mediator should be able to explain your tax choices concerning the child dependency exemption and the federal head-of-household filing status. It helps if your mediator is a good teacher, one who can talk to you in a language you understand, as you will be the ones making the decisions.

Many parents deposit money into an account for a child, called a custodial account. This area is definitely not as complex as many of the divorce topics; however, there are rules concerning such accounts, and mediators are apt to know these rules.

2. OWN A HOUSE

Remember the movie *War of the Roses?* There is a scene where the husband shouts at his wife, "You'll never get the house!" after which the divorcing couple spend the rest of the film arguing over who will get the marital residence. At the end of the movie, the fighting has so escalated that it ends in the bizarre deaths of both husband and wife, finally putting to rest the infamous question, Who gets the house?

Of all the complicated areas of divorce, this one is the most divisive. Therefore, the more expertise your mediator has in both the area of real estate and the emotional stages of divorce, the better served you will be. In the same vein, if your mediator understands the area of capital gains taxes upon the sale or buy-out of the marital residence, you both will be better off. The issue of the home is especially complex on two levels: the strong emotional ties to the house, and the questions concerning complex financial areas, such as the mortgage, equity, lien, title and deed transfer, buy-out, taxable transfers, and basis. You will need experts in every field if your mediator does not have a good understanding of each of these areas. An accountant can provide some of this information, particularly on taxes.

The psychological issues regarding the house are even more daunting. Both spouses often want the house, not only for financial reasons but for strong emotional reasons as well. I often hear responses ranging from, "It was my first house," "It was our first house," "It was mine before I met you," or "I did all of the decorating and made it beautiful," to "I deserve it" or "I can't live without it." A mediator I know introduces the topic of the marital house by describing the Chinese character for "security"—a woman with a roof over her head.

3. PENSIONS AND RETIREMENT PLANS

Though this area doesn't have the same conflict-ridden reputation as the marital residence, it is a complex area in which clients also have emotional ties. As often as women are depicted as psychologically attached to the house, men are as often psychologically attached to their pension plan. In order for a mediator to begin to help, he will need to have a basic knowledge of ERISA, the federal act that applies to pension and retirement plans. Such plans are further complicated because of the wide range and variety of the plans. Some are relatively simple, like an Individual Retirement Account (IRA), while others, called defined benefit plans, are much more complicated. These latter plans generally require an appraisal in order to provide the present value of the pension plan. If you have a pension that you want to divide or transfer, your mediator should know the rules concerning transfer and division. This topic is rife with complicated tax and other rules.

4. AN APARTMENT

Most likely, your mediator will be familiar with whether or not there are any local and/or state tax advantages for apartment occupants. The marital apartment is also a frequent area of conflict, as typically both clients want to remain in the residence and have the other go through the hassle of moving out. Important concerns here, in addition to moving out, are the security deposit and the last month's rent. Who will get these accounts? If one or both plan to move into another apartment, how will the security deposit and the first and last months' rents be handled? What about the apartment contents?

5. MEDICAL AND DENTAL INSURANCE COVERAGE

For many workers, being employees means that they have affordable medical coverage. When a divorce occurs, it is often the case that one spouse may have to obtain his or her own medical insurance coverage. The cost of such individual coverage is often prohibitive or totally beyond reach. Medical coverage has become an important issue in divorce, ranking right up there with child support and division of assets. Federal rules, known as COBRA, kick in at the time of divorce, and these rules require that the ex-spouse be allowed to purchase thirty-six months of health insurance coverage at the cost of an individual plan plus an administration fee. For many of the formerly married, it is crucial to maintain existing coverage and, in many states, this is possible.

Alongside federal laws, many states also have laws concerning medical and dental insurance coverage for an ex-spouse. Couples in these states may be able to continue such coverage for an ex-spouse at the same premium cost of a family plan, even upon divorce. A few states, such as Massachusetts, actually allow for an ex-spouse and a current spouse to continue under the same insurance provider. Such benefits are extremely valuable for an ex-spouse. Though most mediators should be more than familiar with the area of medical health insurance, don't take it for granted. Be sure to check if your mediator is familiar with both medical and dental insurance coverage upon divorce.

6. INVESTMENT ACCOUNTS, STOCKS, BONDS, AND MUTUAL FUNDS

In order to assist with division of assets, your mediator should be able to understand the written documents you provide, to look at an investment account or a mutual fund statement and explain it to you. This is especially necessary if one of the spouses does not have financial expertise. That individual will rely on the mediator to explain financial matters, so that each spouse has enough understanding to make an informed decision.

It will help if the mediator is knowledgeable about subsequent investor topics such as tax basis, nontaxability, and taxability of transfers between spouses. Mediators are more likely to have a basic understanding of the financial investment itself, rather than these tax consequences. If the mediator does not have this kind of tax expertise, an independent tax consultant can help.

7. CREDIT CARD DEBT

Dividing debt is more difficult than dividing assets and, however unfortunate, most people have a significant amount of debt. In fact, professionals in the field of divorce note that the divorcing individual generally has a higher rate of debt than the average consumer. The important issues here are the mediator's understanding of the availability of credit for each spouse, the implication of joint versus individual credit card debt and other debts, joint versus individual liability, and the removal of a name from an account. A good number of mediators will be familiar with these issues.

Good psychological skills in dealing with conflict are important here as well. Neither person wants to walk away with all or most of the debt. The debt brings up their past life together, and lifestyle is an all-too-frequent point of argument. The skilled mediator will be able to help sort out even the most complicated of debt situations.

8. FUTURE COLLEGE PAYMENTS

This is a "maybe" for a lot of parents. Though it's important for a significant number, it's also a matter of financial ability and the ages of your children. If your child is a teenager who knows college is in her future, then a mediator knowledgeable in this area can be a tremendous resource as you can tackle the finances of college without the cost and time of additional experts. Furthermore, if you think that you or your child may require financial aid in order to attend college, a mediator who understands the federal Financial Aid Form (FAF) is worth her weight in gold, though this is also information you can obtain elsewhere—from professional FAF consultants, for example.

9. SELF-EMPLOYED

A self-employed person may work in a vast range of occupational settings. On the one hand, a self-employed music teacher may give lessons two times a week at $10 a lesson; on the other, a self-employed dentist may take in $300,000 per year. Both may file an individual federal tax form called a Schedule C. The mediator should have a basic working knowledge of Schedule C terms and practices: gross income, expenses, deductions, net profit, cost of goods, depreciation, auto and truck expenses, and office in the home. The mediator should be able to understand and explain these expenses. If, however, the spouse has incorporated her business, it becomes a very complex area. Included in this category are single individuals, who incorporate for any number of reasons, to large corporations with complicated asset holdings. Be familiar with the kind of self-employment tax form you or your spouse files; it will allow you to ask the mediator if he is comfortable helping you make an informed decision concerning a business.

10. PROFESSIONAL LICENSE

In some states, a professional license is a marital asset. Once again, you want a mediator who is familiar with the laws in your state. Remember, you cannot divorce yourself. You need a judge to approve your Divorce Agreement and grant you a divorce, and you must file a settlement that is in line with the law in your state.

11. REALTY TRUSTS AND OTHER TRUSTS

The world of trusts is a world unto itself. Trust lawyers are a breed apart, and your mediator will most likely not be an expert in this area, which is acceptable. She needs only to have a basic understanding of trusts in order to draft any provisions of the divorce agreement concerning this issue.

12. OVER AGE 55

Two categories of divorcing couples, in which one or both spouses are over age 55, need specific information from their mediator. The first group are those couples who have a marital residence which, upon a sale, will incur a capital gains tax. Having a mediator who is intimately familiar with the age-55 exclusion could save you thousands of dollars in taxes. The second group will appreciate a mediator who is familiar with benefits for those who are, or will shortly be, concerned with federal Social Security benefits. In the area of Social Security, an important rule allows a woman to receive her own monthly benefit or the equivalent of one-half of her ex-spouse's benefit, whichever is greater, providing she was married to that individual for a minimum of ten years. There is important information in this area, and it may not be every mediator's cup of tea, so ask. The information also can be obtained from your local Social Security office.

13. LACK OF COMMUNICATION BETWEEN SPOUSES

At least several times a day, whether from callers or during a session, I hear from a client that "we can't communicate." It's often true and may be a characteristic of all divorcing couples. During one session, a client Tom turned to his wife and asked, "You said there was mail for me?" His wife responded, "Joyce said you'd be late," to which he replied, "I can't go that night." She answered, "The mail is still there." I had no idea what they were talking about and asked if they wanted my help. Both looked at me as if to say, "See, we don't communicate." When people say this, they are invariably right. A good mediator, one with psychological skills, can make the difference in helping couples to communicate with each other.

14. NOT ENOUGH MONEY TO GO AROUND

If there is one factor that mediators must possess, it is familiarity with the budget. All mediators use a budget as their basic tool, and it is the most important one for reaching agreement concerning financial matters. The more financial expertise a mediator has, the more helpful he will be. A budget is actually a record, typically on a spreadsheet, that lists each person's monthly expenses and income. The budget allows mediators to help clients allocate their often limited amount of money in a manner that each person will deem fair.

15. SUPPORT PAYMENTS (ALIMONY)

Some people call all of their support payments child support, others designate some or all as alimony. For many, the difference is the tax deductibility of alimony for the person who is making these support payments. What does it mean to the recipient, and is it a good idea? Mediators in this area can probably save you significant tax dollars. Ask your mediator if she is familiar with federal and state consequences of support. If she does not have the tax expertise to make the calculation of after-tax income, an accountant can provide you with the appropriate recommendations.

16. ALCOHOL/DRUG ABUSE

People who abuse alcohol or drugs are often unpredictable as clients, as they engage in behavior that is affected by their addiction. If your spouse abuses alcohol or drugs and your mediator does not have a working understanding of the behavior of such individuals, your spouse may very well undermine the mediation. Mediators cannot cure drug or alcohol abuse, but in order to reach a fair settlement they need to understand the dynamics of alcohol and drug abuse. At a minimum, for example, the mediator should know that denial is the primary defense mechanism of most alcoholics.

As mentioned earlier, untreated and severe alcoholics and drug addicts are not appropriate for mediation. If your spouse's alcohol or drug problem is not severe, you will do well to choose a mediator who has not only counseling under his belt, but real-life experience in interacting with that population.

17. DOMESTIC VIOLENCE

Not all mediators are trained in domestic violence. Those mediation organizations that do mandate domestic violence training for their members may require only a one- or two-hour educational workshop. For someone unfamiliar with the dangers posed by domestic violence, this may not be adequate. The best choice for a mediator in such cases is one who has had substantial experience in this field, perhaps, for example, one who has worked on a hotline for battered women or as a therapist with men who batter, and who has taken several educational training seminars. It is most important that your mediator know about safety issues for victims of domestic violence, have support references (the ability to provide the name of the nearest support person, as well as a group for perpetrators), and is clear on the legal issues surrounding such violence. Most important, the mediator must understand power differences, though this ability may be difficult for you to discern even when you're sitting in the room with them. If there is an existing restraining order, make sure that the mediator is aware of it, so that special arrangements can be made for the sessions.

18. REFUSAL TO PAY CHILD SUPPORT

If one of you is already stating that the other is refusing to pay child support, you'll need a mediator who is very familiar with two areas: your state's statute concerning child support, and the specific practices in the divorce court where your hearing will be held. This is common information known by divorce lawyers, but a good nonlawyer mediator will also be aware of it. The information also may be obtained by independent, consulting attorneys.

19. UNUSUAL PARENTING ARRANGEMENTS/ DIVISION OF ASSETS

In order to be granted a divorce a judge must approve your agreement. The more your agreement falls within the parameters of "usual," the more likely the judge will be to approve it. To know what is typical for your case, your mediator should be able to offer guidelines, but if you want a judge to approve an arrangement that differs from the norm, it is helpful to know in advance how the judge tends to rule in such cases. The mediator should be able to help with this, though she may refer you to a divorce lawyer if your agreement, is outside the range of a usual divorce settlement.

20. MINIMAL FUNDS

If the payment of mediation fees is a problem, you may be well served by a mediator who will do at least one of the following: make available a sliding-fee scale (mediation fees based on the client's ability to pay), negotiate the mediation fees, accept your case on a pro bono basis (which means free), or offer a payment plan. Discuss fees and payment plans during your first call and/or during the introductory session. It's never too soon to discuss money.

21. A HIGH-CONFLICT COUPLE/VERY ARGUMENTATIVE

Your mediator can also help if you and your spouse are arguing, or if one or both is hostile or withdrawn. Mediation skills are designed to reduce anger and hostility, engage the withdrawn client, and allow you to communicate with each other. People often think that aggressive clients are the most difficult to deal with during a mediation session. That's not true for me and for many of the mediators I know. Instead, it is the passive or withdrawn individual who is the most difficult. With this type of personality, one needs a mediator who not only has good mediation skills but who can engage an individual.

Even if you have already started to disagree with each other, don't despair. A mediator's classic expertise is in helping you to resolve your dispute. The best evidence here is your own gut reaction to a potential mediator. Inevitably, couples will disagree over some issue during their introductory session. It's difficult, but while you are arguing during or after the session, remember how the mediation went. Did you feel helped? Did you think she was neutral? Did you get a chance to talk? Did you feel that he listened to you? The last factor is extremely important, perhaps more than anything else. You need a mediator who is not biased. Follow your feelings—they are a good sign.

• • •

This list is not a road map—you do not need to, nor could you, fulfill every point. It would be unlikely to find all of those qualifications in one person. Instead, choose the mediator characteristics that will most help you with your top priority issues.

5

Generating Names
of Potential Mediators

The first place to begin your research is with the
Academy of Family Mediators' state-by-state list
of Practitioner Members, on page 131. It is the
most recent list available at this writing. If you want to check
whether a name is current, or if you want more information,
you can write or call the AFM at 4 Militia Drive, Lexington, MA
02173; (617) 674-2663.

If you don't find anyone listed in your town (and depending on where you live, that may well be the case), don't automatically rule out someone in another part of your state or
in a neighboring state. Even if it requires some traveling on
your part, it will be worth it to get the services of a competent
mediator.

Even if you do find a name on the list, you should not consider your search to be over. Remember, this list is merely a
place to begin. You still need to find out whether or not that mediator has all the qualifications you need. Chapter 7 provides a
list of questions to ask on your initial telephone call—and don't
forget to request his or her written material, which describes the
practice and provides additional necessary information.

If you do not find a mediator on the Practitioner list (and
even if you do, I advise putting together a list of from three to

six names), another likely place to find names is in the Yellow Pages, where a lot of couples begin. In other kinds of advertising, people may advise you to choose someone who is using a simple line listing: "Don't pay attention to the expensive display ads." But in this profession, my recommendation is the opposite. I'd suggest that you call first those who advertise with a big ad, specifically those that provide the name of the mediator. Display ads cost more than line ads, which may mean that the professional is willing to invest in mediation advertising. You may increase your chances of reaching someone who does a substantial amount of mediation. It's not a guarantee, but it makes sense. Choose three or four names, call them, and ask to speak to the mediators. If they are not available, ask that they return your call. If they call back, they've passed one hurdle. If they don't call back in a reasonable period of time, say two days, cross them off the list.

Some clients explain that they were referred to me when they told their friends and co-workers that they were looking for a mediator. Don't wait for people to find you to provide you with the name of a mediator. It's up to you to ask, to put out the word. This may not be easy. During the early stages of separation, most people, especially the person being left, do not want anyone to know about it, which makes it difficult to tell people about the break-up in the hope of getting the name of a mediator. Yet, if you don't tell, there is no possibility of getting a referral. So, be brave, take a deep breath, and tell your friends. Many people will be impressed by your seeking the services of a mediator. And a little respect from your friends will do your ego good during this vulnerable time.

Another way to begin your search is by calling a divorce attorney or a therapist, as these are the two professions with the most contact with mediators. Certified Public Accountants and tax preparers may also be resources. Although they are not as likely to know mediators, they are still worth a try. Call and explain that you are seeking a mediator and would appreciate a referral. Generally, professionals are glad to accommodate you in the hope that you will call again if you require their services. There's no cost to the professional, and it generates goodwill.

A common way people receive referrals in any area is remembering a friend who used a professional, and then contacting the friend for the name. In mediation, however, this process doesn't always work as well. Litigation clients often complain loudly about the trauma and expense of the adversarial process. Mediated clients reach divorce agreements outside of the public eye. Of course, mediated clients must still go to court for a divorce hearing; however, their disputes are not aired out at a public court hearing, as the settlement has already been reached, and thus the court process is routine. Since mediation clients value privacy and because it is not a destructive process, clients are less apt to describe their use of the mediation process. As a rule, people talk about a service if it's wildly fantastic (not many services fit that description) or if they are dissatisfied with it. Consequently, people bandy about the names of divorce lawyers, but the same isn't as likely for divorce mediators. Still, think of people you know who have gone through a divorce. Some may have used a mediator or know someone else who did.

Other places to obtain referrals are organizations that have some association with divorce or with single parents. Listings of divorce groups can be found at many churches as well as at therapists' offices. There are often announcements for groups in your local paper. Parents Without Partners is a well-run group offering support to single parents. If your town has a community mediation organization, it may have a list of private divorce mediators. The mediation organization can most likely be found by looking in your local telephone book or newspaper. Local and state bar associations may provide names of mediators; however, most may be attorneys who practice different kinds of law rather than attorneys who practice mediation. Your local and state professional association of therapists and psychologists may have listings, and they should be good referrals. And the Internet also offers a rich place to search for mediation organizations. Look under http://www.igc.apc.org/conflictnet.

An excellent resource is your state or local mediation organizations. If states certify or license mediators, they generally have referral lists. If they do not, mediator associations may also have referral lists that provide the names of mediators in your area. However, these organizations may be difficult to track down because they often do not do much advertising. Look in the telephone book or call the American Arbitration Association.

A court might be able to give you a name: You may be invited to use a court mediator, or in some areas, the court will provide you with a list of private mediators, especially in those states that certify mediators. If you do contact a court, it must be a family or a probate court, not just any kind of court. Not all courts have mediators, and not all states have them.

Let me provide some background concerning court mediators. A person who is employed by a court or who volunteers in a court-connected program is often called a court mediator. However, do not let that label lull you into a false sense of having found your divorce mediator. There is a world of difference between a public and a private mediator. A private mediator has no authority over her clients, nor can she impose a decision upon you. Even more significant, she cannot make a recommendation to the court. A private mediator keeps what you say confidential, unless there is a specific law requiring notification (which might occur in the case of sexual abuse of a minor). And a private mediator can be terminated at your will. Court mediators work very differently. They are mainly evaluators or investigators, though they may mediate disputes as well. This may sound unbelievable, but it is absolutely possible for a husband and wife to reach an agreement and yet have a court mediator substitute his own idea for the settlement. Typically, the court mediator has the power to recommend a settlement to the court, removing your control over your decisions. Though you may like some solutions, most likely you won't like others. Yet once you are locked into the court system, it is very difficult to get out. With a court mediator, you give up your ability to terminate. You give up your autonomy.

Several states have "mandatory mediation," which means that couples who are marked up on the court docket for a contested issue (a disagreement concerning their separation or divorce) are required to see a court mediator. Though using a public mediator is certainly better than going to trial, my advice is to seek the services of a private mediator at the start of your divorce negotiations, so you don't end up being forced to use a court mediator.

You also may be referred to an organization of community mediators. Within the profession, community mediators are considered to be a different breed from private mediators. During the 1970s, about the same time that divorce mediation began, a parallel type of mediation developed. The theory underlying community mediation is that mediators come from the community in which the conflict took place—peers mediate their peers. Community mediators are generally not experts in the specific type of disputes at hand. For example, many years ago I was a community mediator with a Massachusetts Community Mediation Center, and when I mediated landlord/tenant disagreements, I was not familiar with the laws concerning the rights and obligations of landlords or tenants. Though this type of mediation works fine with minor disputes, it is not appropriate in the area of divorce. It is possible, of course, that the community mediator in question is an expert in the area of divorce, though this is not typical. Community mediators, however, may be able to refer you to a private divorce mediator.

Another way to generate the name of a mediator is through your employer. If your company has an Employment Assistance Program (EAP), it usually includes referrals for professional services. There may be the name of a good mediator on file.

I'd like to be able to list the clergy as a good referral source, but up to now, they have seemed to avoid gathering that kind of information. They are a good source for finding a divorce support group, and the group facilitator may be able to provide a referral to a mediator. There are a few exceptions, however; the Catholic Paulist Center and the Unitarian Universalist clergy take a more active role in sponsoring groups for people separating and divorcing. It is hoped that many more clergy will become knowledgeable about divorce services, since many men and women often turn to their priests, ministers, and rabbis for help at such times.

Approaching a number of sources for referrals is a good idea, because if a specific mediator's name keeps coming up, it's a good indication that he or she is well respected. In the field of mediation, reputations are hard-won and if a number of people point to a specific mediator, it's a good sign. But still try to gather several names. I suggest an initial list of three to six, which you'll begin to whittle down, based on responses.

6

Interviewing Mediators: Questions to Ask

The interview is the most important step in choosing a good mediator. The burden of finding a good one is on the client—you. I recommend that you have three preliminary interview contacts with a potential mediator. All three needn't be in person, but at least one should be face to face. I advise the following sequence: the initial telephone conversation, your review of the mediation information, and a personal interview at the time of the introductory session. A word to the impatient: Don't skip the introductory session, even if you feel 100 percent positive that you'll choose this individual. Consider the initial appointment as the foundation of your mediation, and treat it accordingly. The point of each of these contacts is to gather information to help you to decide the two important points in choosing a mediator: competency and suitability to your situation.

Here is a suggested list of questions to ask to determine if the mediator is competent.

MEDIATOR COMPETENCY QUESTIONS

1. How long have you been mediating divorce cases?
2. How many times do you mediate during one week?
3. What other types of mediations do you do?
4. Where did you receive training? Was it an Academy of Family Mediators–approved training?
5. What additional training and/or supervision have you had?
6. Are you an AFM Practitioner or General member? If yes, since when? To what other mediation organizations do you belong, if any?
7. What is your educational and professional background?
8. Are you certified as a mediator? By which organization?
9. Are you licensed in a profession? Which profession, and by whom? How long have you been licensed? Have there ever been any problems with your licensing?
10. What percentage of your practice is mediation?
11. Do you subscribe to any organization standards?

MEDIATION PROCEDURE QUESTIONS

12. Do you have a mediation packet to send?
13. Do you provide a free introductory session? May my spouse also talk to you before our first session?
14. Do you mediate alone? With a co-mediator or a team? Are there additional mediators who work in your office? If yes, who chooses which mediator we use?
15. Do you meet with both of us together at all sessions?
16. Do you require each of us to consult with or retain a lawyer?
17. Do you give information on each divorce topic or will we still need an expert to give us that information?
18. What are your fees, and are they payable at our first ses-

sion? Do you charge a retainer, and is it payable at our first session? What forms of payment do you accept? Do you offer a sliding scale?

19. What mediation appointment times are available? Do you have evening/weekend hours?
20. Will we be expected to sign a mediation contract? When? Can we get a copy of it?
21. Can you give me the names of at least two other good mediators in the area who know you and will attest to your competence?

I realize that many of you will look at this list and shake your head in disbelief. Granted, it is long, but my intent is to make it comprehensive. Remember that the Mediator Competency Questions are the most important. Pay attention to these first eleven questions. Furthermore, the first four questions should be asked over the telephone, during the initial contact, and the remaining seven questions during the introductory session. Writing them down may prove helpful.

Let's look at the preferred responses to the first set of questions on Mediator Competency.

1. How long have you been mediating divorce cases?

Your mediator should have a minimum of three to five years of divorce mediation experience. Less than that, and you are getting a novice. If a novice is okay with you, you may want the assurance that there is a mediator consultant or a supervisor in the wings. My preference is that a mediator have at least five years' experience and that all of the experience be in the area of divorce. Other types of mediation experience are a plus, but I would not substitute them for divorce experience. For example, if someone has ten years' experience in mediating insurance claims, that would not be the equivalent of five years of divorce mediation. Divorce is very different from other types of mediation.

If you know you and your spouse are a couple who have a high degree of conflict or intense power struggles, you may opt for a mediator with even more experience—someone with eight or more years in the field would be best. Over the years, callers have complained that they could not find an experienced mediator geographically convenient to them. I consistently advise the callers that it is worth the travel to find a good mediator. Today, unfortunately, it is still true that good mediators are few and far between.

This first question addresses only one part of mediator experience. The response to the next question provides the additional information you need in order to determine the validity of the mediator's experience, and therefore is a necessary follow-up.

2. *How many times do you mediate during one week?*

You may be surprised if a mediator tells you that she has several years' experience in mediation yet she does only three or four mediations during an entire year. This is not an adequate number. Instead, I would choose a mediator with a minimum of three mediations per week if her response is to be a meaningful indicator of experience. Be persistent in seeking out an actual number of sessions per week. If the potential mediator insists that she can't give you an exact number, ask for an educated guess. As a general rule, the more mediations per week, the more experience she has, which should translate into the better her expertise. For a comparison, I typically do three mediations a day, though sometimes I may do only two and occasionally as many as four. It is not unusual for a full-time professional to do one or two mediations a day.

3. *What other types of mediations do you do?*

If you are seeking a mediator to help you with your separation or divorce, then someone who has done only commercial mediation will not be helpful. As in most other specialties, you need a professional who has the appropriate background. In the same way that you wouldn't consult with a brain surgeon if you had a problem with your foot, you need someone who is a family or divorce mediator, one well versed in the intricacies of divorce law, finances, and custody. I recognize that the word *family* may be misleading to some, but it is standard use in the field of divorce, derived from the legal system's use of the word.

4. Where did you receive training? Was it an Academy of Family Mediators–approved training?

This will be a difficult response for you to evaluate unless you know a little about training programs in general, and the approved programs in particular. There are no national requirements for training and, as far I know, little or no individual state requirements for the trainers. Anyone can do almost any kind of training and call it divorce mediation training. Because of the total lack of guidelines in this field, you'll do best to rely on a reliable organization that has set mediation training standards. The Academy of Family Mediators (AFM), a well-known organization in the field of divorce mediation, is primarily comprised of divorce mediators in private practice. I was president of AFM from 1995 to 1996 and a board member when the standards for training programs were developed. These standards have become the accepted model for training programs throughout the country. Basic training for all divorce mediators is a forty-hour program. AFM continues to approve basic and advanced divorce mediation trainings and maintains a list of all approved training programs. You may call the AFM at (800) 292-4AFM, and they will tell you if a training program has been AFM-approved. Be sure to remember to ask the potential mediator the names of his trainers so you can verify those names with the AFM list.

If the training is not AFM-approved, I'd be hesitant to use this mediator unless I knew a lot more about his professional skills. If you want to pursue this mediator regardless, you might consider asking another mediator about him. Taking a training course shows that he has a willingness to learn, to be open to new and different ideas, and to be willing to take constructive criticism.

If the mediator admits that he has had no training, I'd immediately cross him off my list. Every mediator needs training. Mediation is a skill. If, somehow, you are considering one of the first mediators in the country who started twenty years ago, when there was no training available, I'd still require training! It's never too late to pursue further training, and he could have taken at least one course over the years.

5. What additional training and/or supervision have you had?

As a general rule, the more training your mediator has had, the more expertise she has. I would want a mediator to have at least one hundred hours of training in addition to the basic forty-hour mediation course, though my preference is for closer to five to six hundred hours of training. The few academic programs that do exist, such as those at the University of Massachusetts and Antioch College, concentrate on dispute resolution or negotiation. Academic programs differ greatly from mediation training ones, as the former stress theoretical foundation while the latter are primarily experiential.

Training should not be limited to the mediation process, but rather should include the substantive areas of divorce. Substantive means the particular knowledge within a field. For example, if someone has substantive knowledge of child support, she would know the child support guidelines for your state and the laws concerning such issues, such as the amount, whether wage assignment is available, and the length of time that such support is required by law. If a mediator has no training in this substantive area, she could not provide the basic information you'd need in order to make informed decisions. There are many complex areas of divorce, such as real estate, pensions, and insurance, in which you'll want your mediator to have considerable knowledge.

6. Are you an AFM Practitioner or General member?
If yes, since when? To what other mediation
organizations do you belong, if any?

As already mentioned, AFM is a national organization with two categories of membership, Practitioner and General. Anyone who sends in the annual fee can be a General member, so if I had a choice, I'd choose a Practitioner member. To qualify for this category, a mediator must complete a minimum of sixty hours of training, one hundred hours of face-to-face mediation, submission of written documents, and continuing-education credit. Just as important, the qualification demonstrates that he is interested in being held accountable to a professional organization of private divorce mediators. Remember, none of the responses I'm advising you to seek out are guarantees of a competent mediator, but are rather signposts.

Once a mediator has been approved as a Practitioner member of AFM, he can apply to be an Academy Consultant, who is required to have substantially more training and experience. As AFM Consultants are few, you need not necessarily seek one as your mediator, although it is certainly a sign of a very experienced professional.

In addition to AFM, there are other national professional organizations. The Association of Family and Conciliation Courts (AFCC) is a national organization composed primarily of court-connected people. Members are mostly judges, lawyers, court workers, guardians ad litem (those appointed by the court to look out for the best interests of the child or children), and a host of other individuals who work with families involved with the court system. Though there are not a substantial number of private mediators within this organization, there are some.

SPDR (pronounced "spider") is the Society of Professionals in Dispute Resolution, an organization composed of varied kinds of neutrals, or professionals who help to resolve disputes, and includes mediators, arbitrators, and conciliators. In the future, this organization may offer regulation or certification for its members.

There is also the American Arbitration Association, called Triple A, which includes neutrals who practice mediation.

AFCC, Triple A, SPDR, and AFM are the primary organizations of professionals who practice as dispute resolvers. However, only AFM has requirements of its members, which help you determine competency. Canadian residents will encounter professionals involved with a very active organization called Family Mediation Canada (FMC), comprised of a substantial number of private mediators.

7. *What is your educational and professional background?*

I know a well-respected divorce mediator who holds a master's degree in electrical engineering. After starting a practice as a divorce mediator, he then went on to school and obtained a master's degree in social work. "I did it," he says, "because I know I needed that kind of academic education in dealing with people." Don't undervalue an academic degree. An educational background does provide some indication of the qualities you'll want in a mediator.

Some people argue that a professional degree is not necessarily a clear indication of a good mediator. I wholeheartedly agree with that statement. Education alone is not proof of competency. However, the successful attainment of a degree, particularly an advanced degree, does indicate an ability for intellectual accomplishment, perseverance, and knowledge in that field, as well as a professional attitude. This is no small point. An academic degree is simply one more signpost to a good mediator, and it is one that I would want in a professional

I hire. I recommend that you look for a mediator who holds an advanced educational degree, such as a master's, a Ph.D., or a Juris doctorate, not simply an undergraduate degree. Educational backgrounds I'd look for in a divorce mediator include graduate degrees in law, social work, psychology, dispute resolution, and possibly business or taxation.

A professional degree in mediation or dispute resolution is new. As of this writing, two universities (the University of Massachusetts and Antioch College) have begun master's programs in dispute resolution, and these programs may become more popular in the future. Education will provide more qualified professionals, which should help consumers.

In addition, many professionals are cross-trained, or have more than one graduate degree. Though it is rare to find a blend of the three significant areas of divorce mediation, a substantial number of mediators have two of the three areas of law, psychology, and finance. If you are looking for someone who is cross-trained, do not be shy about asking. The more training and experience in each of these three areas your mediator has, the better for you.

8. Are you certified as a mediator? By which organization?

As mentioned earlier, some states are just now starting to certify mediators. If your particular state does, you will want to choose someone who is certified. Beware, though, not to rely on the label alone. Certification is a minimum standard. Although it does provide evidence that your mediator has complied with the required guidelines, you will want more information than this label provides.

If the potential mediator responds yes, s/he is certified, you need to follow up with, "By which organization?" This is very important. At a minimum, after you are given the name of the organization, ask for the address and phone number and the name of its executive director. In many states, the certifying group is a private organization, rather than state-run, and you'll want to know their requirements for certification.

If the mediator cannot provide adequate information to enable you to contact the certifying organization, continue your search.

Once you contact the organization, ask for a list of its members, as well as its requirements for certification. Review these requirements carefully. If they aren't clear to you, bring them up with your potential mediator. This will be a reliable preview to the manner in which she will answer your questions once you're in mediation, when you're bound to have many.

9. Are you licensed in a profession?
Which profession, and by whom?
How long have you been licensed?
Have there ever been any problems with your licensing?

Most mediators have had prior professional lives, such as lawyers or therapists. However, if someone tells you that he was an insurance agent or a hair dresser prior to starting mediation, with the utmost respect to those professions, you'd better ask a lot of questions or look elsewhere. If the individual has another profession in addition to his mediation practice, you may want to ask if he maintains his license in that other area of practice. This is important because it is possible that he may have had professional difficulties in a prior profession, such as disbarment from practice, which you'd want to know.

10. What percentage of your practice is mediation?

If the potential mediator holds a license in a profession and continues to practice, find out how much time she spends in comparison to her mediation work. Does she do only one or two mediations per year while working full-time as a therapist?

Obviously, the more time she spends mediating, the better qualified she is to do so.

11. Do you subscribe to any organization standards?

Most mediation organizations have standards, written guidelines for the practice. Find out to which professional mediation standards the mediator subscribes. Ask for a copy of the standards. If there are no standards, I'd be wary.

• • •

While the next set of questions are not as important as those above, the responses will assist you in narrowing down the mediators appropriate for you, as they concern the practicalities of price and the like.

MEDIATION PROCEDURE QUESTIONS

12. Do you have a mediation packet to send?

All mediators I have met send their potential clients free written information prior to their first session. The material may vary greatly—from a simple, one-page brochure to a comprehensive notebook of services. Review the material carefully. This is the mediator's best foot forward.

I suggest requesting packets from at least three mediators, and as many as five or six. Read through each to note what is of interest to you.

If you haven't yet told your spouse of your intentions, or if you don't want your neighborhood mail carrier to know of your impending divorce, ask if the information packet is sent without the word *divorce* on the envelope. It's a plus if your mediator is thoughtful enough not to put it there. If the mediators don't have a free information packet, I would ask why and weigh their response thoughtfully.

13. Do you provide a free introductory session?
May my spouse also talk to you before our first session?

Most, but not all, of the mediators I know offer a free introductory session. As explained earlier, the purpose of the session is to allow the mediator to explain the process to potential clients and to allow the clients to ask questions and assess the mediator's qualifications.

There is no standard length of time for that free introductory session. I offer thirty-minute sessions; some are as short as fifteen minutes. Some couples erroneously assume that they can discuss their disagreements or otherwise work on their divorce settlement during that period. This is not what usually occurs during an introductory session. Whether or not a mediator offers a free introductory session is certainly not determinative of a good mediator. I provide a free session because I think clients value it and it is a good way for me to explain the process at my time and expense, not theirs. But as a client, you can certainly obtain the same information by paying for the mediation time. And remember, you can always ask the mediator if s/he would provide a free introductory session, even if it is not common practice.

A mediator should encourage, or at least agree to, your spouse's calling prior to the first session. Remember, the mediator must be neutral and not take sides. If a mediator declines to talk with your spouse prior to the mediation session without providing a very good reason, it's probably a good sign to steer clear.

Please note that the mediator *cannot* call your spouse. That is considered solicitation, and it is unprofessional. However, you can ask your spouse to call her.

When I first started, I assumed I would speak with both spouses on the telephone before I met with them together.

Sixteen-plus years later, I know better. Typically, I speak with only one spouse prior to the introductory session, though I'd prefer to speak to both and offer to do so in the written material I send out as well as during that initial call. It's rare for the other spouse to call, but I still think it's a good idea.

14. Do you mediate alone? With a co-mediator or a team?
Are there additional mediators who work in your office?
If yes, who chooses which mediator we use?

Most divorce mediators work alone. However, there are exceptions. Some work in teams, while others work in partnerships. Usually, team mediation consists of two mediators during a session, but the total number of mediators on the panel may number from three to twelve or more, and from that panel, either you will choose two or two will be assigned to your case. These mediators work together in various combinations, though each may specialize in one area. Sometimes, the same mediators remain with a case throughout its duration, while other teams use different combinations of mediators throughout the sessions,

Mediators who work in a partnership are somewhat more common than teams. Usually, co-mediator partnerships consist of one male and one female mediator, ostensibly to reflect the gender division in the room. The alleged advantage of this co-mediator team is that the husband has his ally and the wife her ally. As you may surmise, I do not endorse this arrangement. Though I understand the supposed benefit, I question whether it is actually a benefit, since it may lead to the appearance of an adversarial setting in which the male client looks to the male mediator for support while the female client looks to the female mediator. This same gender arrangement may escalate the division between the respective clients and, just as important, negate the importance of mediator neutrality. (I discuss the gender factor in more detail in chapter 7.)

My concern with having two mediators in the room comes from my background and experience as a therapist. As someone who was trained to understand interpersonal dynamics, I can provide a general rule: The more people in a room, the more interaction there is among those people. To be specific, if you have one mediator, there are three interactions; one between mediator and husband, another between mediator and wife, and a third between husband and wife. However, if you add another mediator, you double the interactions to six. Let me illustrate with a diagram:

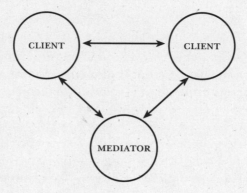

Two mediators and two clients:

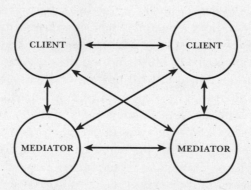

With two mediators in the room, the interpersonal dynamics become significantly more complex. Mediation can certainly take place with more than one mediator, but it takes greater skill on the part of each, and it helps if both have a strong background in psychology.

In my opinion, the disadvantages of gender pairing outweigh the benefits. Mediation is not about men versus women, or one side versus the other. Mediation needs to be a cooperative venture, to help a divorcing couple work together to resolve the impasse and reach agreement. I think it makes sense to use one neutral mediator.

If there is a panel of mediators in the office from which to choose, ask for the qualifications and fees charged for each, and ask whether you may choose the person or if the office staff assigns one. Mediation effectiveness is heavily dependent on the specific mediator, so if you are willing to do some homework on the players, it is best if you are the one who does the choosing. I would choose the best mediator in the office, regardless of cost or convenience.

15. *Do you meet with both of us together at all sessions?*

A divorce mediator typically meets with both the husband and wife together, unless there is a reason not to, as when domestic violence is involved.

If the mediator begins by wanting to meet separately with you (called a caucus), it may have several implications: The mediator may not do a substantial amount of family mediation and may be more comfortable working with one client at a time; she is screening for domestic violence; or she was not trained in the traditional divorce mediation model. The best way for you to deal with a mediator who wants to mediate separately is to ask why. You should feel satisfied with the explanation. Other than for screening purposes, I have a strong preference for a mediator who works with both clients in the same room.

If the mediator does want to caucus, and if you agree to do so, be certain to ask about confidentiality. Is what you say to the mediator during the caucus confidential, or will she tell your spouse what you've said? Be clear on this point from the start. There is

no universal rule that requires a mediator to be confidential—
every state is different.

16. Do you require each of us to consult with or to retain a lawyer?

Prior to engaging a mediator, you will want to know if he will require you to consult an attorney or whether it will be your decision to do so. I'd also want to know if he will refer you to specific
attorneys. (This knowledge is helpful for a number of reasons,
discussed in chapter 8.)

Most mediators I know request that each client consult with
an independent, separate attorney prior to signing the final
document. There are clients who choose not to do so, some because they dislike attorneys, some because they don't want to
spend the money, and others philosophically see attorney consults as inconsistent with the mediation process.

If you or your spouse falls into one of these categories, it may
be helpful to you to use a mediator who is a lawyer. No mediator
can act as a lawyer, but it will help ensure that he is knowledgeable about legal issues. Nonlawyer mediators can be just as
knowledgeable about all of the legal issues in divorce, but it may
be difficult for you to ascertain such information.

17. Do you give information on each divorce topic or will we still need an expert to give us that information?

I cannot overemphasize the importance of this question. The
mediator should have a basic understanding of all the major
substantive areas of divorce and should also be familiar with the
divorce court you'll be going to. For example, does the mediator
understand tax issues, or will each of you need to see an accountant in order to reach tax agreements for your divorce settlement? If your assets will include investment accounts, will you
each be required to consult a financial advisor? Does the mediator understand the laws on pension transfers, or will she refer

you to someone else? A mediator's expertise is a crucial factor in considering the costs of your mediation. Ask your mediator if there are areas in which she will have to refer you out because she does not provide information on that topic. You don't want any surprises after you've started.

In terms of the divorce settlement, a mediator who understands the complex pension and retirement plans and transfers is recommended. She should know both state and federal laws concerning medical, life, and disability insurance. If you have a child, choose a mediator who is familiar with workable parenting plans and has a knowledge of all factors of support issues. Most difficult to find, though a definite added benefit, is a mediator with the ability to translate the infamous tax consequences of divorce, though this skill is not a requirement. The best mediator has all of this information in order to provide you with possible choices, especially concerning child support guidelines, real estate choices, the pension as an asset, and health insurance laws.

18. What are your fees, and are they payable at our first session? Do you charge a retainer, and is it payable at our first session? What forms of payment do you accept? Do you offer a sliding scale?

Ask about mediation fees upfront. You don't want any surprises later in the process. Before you schedule an appointment, ask the mediator his hourly rate and the average number of sessions required, as well as the length of each session. Ask if there is an additional charge for the written document the mediator drafts. What about telephone calls? Are there additional charges when the mediator reviews the documentation? These are all legitimate and necessary charges, and you'll want a realistic idea of the total fee. Find out what other services have a fee, and what it is.

Ask the mediator if he requires a retainer, or a sum of money for future services, which is paid in advance. For example, if a mediator charges $150 per hour, he may require a retainer of $1,500, an advance for ten hours of work. A mediator who is also a lawyer is more apt to charge a retainer than is a nonlawyer mediator, though this isn't a hard-and-fast rule. And you'll want to know if the mediator wants his retainer at the first visit. I do not require a retainer, and in fact, I won't take one. I reason that if the clients pay as they mediate (at the end of each session), it allows them to have control over the mediation process and makes it truly voluntary. Those mediators who charge retainers defend the practice by explaining that they return any unused portion. Indeed, that may be true, but it takes some discussion and paperwork, all controlled by the mediator, who is holding your money. So, if I were a client, I'd choose a mediator who charges you as you go. However, if all else about the mediator is good, then I would attempt to negotiate, explaining my thinking and hoping he would accept a pay-as-you-go arrangement.

Many mediators have payment plans available. If you want such a plan, ask for it. Don't wait for the mediator to offer one. Even if he doesn't initiate the idea, he may be willing to accept it. Take the lead and suggest the kind of payment schedule you'd prefer. Don't hesitate to be specific.

Some mediators, primarily those who have formerly worked as therapists, offer a sliding scale payment plan. This type of fee structure bases the mediation fee on your income. For example, if the sliding scale is $75 to $125, the more you make, the more you will pay toward the higher end of the fee scale. The less you make, the less you pay. If neither of you earns much money, a sliding scale can make a big difference in the cost of the services.

Mediator's fees vary significantly. Across the country, I'm personally familiar with fees that range from $45 per hour in Tennessee to $375 per hour in New York City, and I wouldn't be surprised to find that the range was even more extreme. Attorney mediators and those with more experience tend to charge more than nonattorney mediators and those newly practicing.

In large urban areas, expect to pay between $150 and $250 per hour. In more rural areas, I'd be surprised if you had to pay more than $100 per hour. Keep in mind that a competent mediator is worth the money. An incompetent mediator will cost you more in the end.

Also find out what forms of payment the mediator accepts. If you want to pay with a credit card, you'll need someone who accepts that form of payment. Not many do. (Our office began accepting Visa and MasterCard only two years ago.)

19. What mediation appointment times are available? Do you have evening/weekend hours?

You may not have the flexibility to take time off from work to attend mediation sessions; therefore, a mediator with accommodating evening or weekend hours may be a necessity for you. Once again, be assertive in describing your needs.

If you get off of work at five P.M. and her last appointment is at five P.M., ask if she could give you a 5:30 or 6:00 appointment. And make sure she'll give you that time for the next sessions as well.

20. Will we be expected to sign a mediation contract? When? Can we get a copy of it?

All mediators should ask you to sign a contract. Ask to have it sent to you prior to the session, if possible. If the mediator presents it to you at the introductory session, you should have time to read it carefully before signing it, and preferably be able to take it home. No mediator should require you to sign a document on the spot, and I'd pass on anyone who asked for my immediate signature. Mediation is an information-getting process, with time allotted for making informed decisions. You want a mediator whose practice exemplifies that definition. Read the contract; if you cannot understand it or if it is not written clearly, ask the mediator to explain it or change it until you are satisfied.

As an aside, the mediation contract should be in English! If it reads like legalese, which means that you'd need a lawyer to interpret it, I'd wonder about the mediator. The contract is a telling first sign.

21. Can you give me the names of at least two other good mediators in the area who know you and will attest to your competence?

Of all of the questions on the list, this may be the single most important. It might sound a little unusual—and I'll grant that it is—yet it allows for a very telling response. In just about every community I know of, the actual number of mediators is small, so a practicing mediator knows or has at least heard of everyone else in the field. A divorce mediator knows who is good and who isn't. If a mediator provides you with the names of other mediators, it indicates that he is in contact with other mediators and he's not so desperate for business that he'll deny knowing others. Most likely, no one will volunteer that another mediator is so exceptional that you should use him, but talking with various mediators gives you a feel for the weaknesses and strengths of each (keeping in mind that each mediator will be marketing himself!). Don't be shy when asking questions concerning another mediator.

Another way to approach this issue is if you already have the names of at least two mediators. Call one and say, "I have the name of another [or two or three] mediator[s] and would like to run them by you for your comments." Listen carefully to the responses. Not only will you find out something about the other mediators, but the person you are talking with will be giving away information about himself.

In addition to getting satisfactory answers to all of these questions, be alert to these qualities in the mediator you decide to choose:

- A respectful attitude
- An ability to respond satisfactorily to your questions
- A willingness to give each person equal opportunity to take part in the sessions
- An unbiased attitude toward you and your spouse

You should feel that your mediator is competent and trustworthy. If some aspect of the process as he or she explains it doesn't sound right, question it. Choose someone whom you feel you can work with. This may seem a time-consuming process, but I believe it is better to spend the time upfront rather than to find yourself with an incompetent mediator. Asking the questions listed here will help you to find the right mediator for you.

7

The Unavoidable Question:
The Gender of the Mediator

An often unspoken question for all divorcing men and women is, "Does the gender of the mediator make a difference?" For a significant number, it does. The reason is the belief in "gender bias"—the idea that a mediator will act a certain way because of his or her gender. Divorcing women often insist on having a female mediator, believing that she will not take the side of a man against a woman. Sometimes, though, a woman seeks a male mediator because she believes that he will side with a woman in order to protect her. Though some men express a strong desire for a male mediator, thinking that he will not be against a male client, many men prefer a female mediator. They may find it easier to talk to a woman or may think she will be less aggressive, according to gender stereotype. Each divorcing individual has his or her reasons, but those who prefer a mediator of one gender or the other share a common underlying belief that the mediator will take sides based on gender.

By definition, a mediator is called a neutral, one who does not take sides. A mediator should never make a conscious decision to take one person's side against the other. If this side taking was evident during mediation, it would be such an obvious breach of professionalism that the whole process would come to a halt. Recently, a fairly new mediator requested a consultation with me and explained her difficulty in mediating with a couple who was arguing bitterly over custody of their seven-year-old daughter. At the end of an argumentative and fruitless session, the mediator told me that she mistakenly blurted out, "I think a growing girl should always remain with her mother, though her dad should have an important role in her care." The father became visibly upset, telling the mediator that she had given an opinion and taken sides, and he refused to continue the process. In addition, the mediator was surprised by the reaction of the wife toward her. She was angry because she felt that the mediator had destroyed her chances of mediating, and now she feared litigation. She told the mediator that she too thought the comment inappropriate and that although she had taken her side, she knew it was wrong for her to do that because a mediator was supposed to be neutral.

It is difficult to regain neutrality after losing it. The mediator's breach of her role compromised the process.

Most divorcing clients, however, rather than having a fear of a mediator blatantly taking one person's side against the other, as in the prior example, worry about a mediator's unconscious or subtle bias. They may assume that the mediator will side with one sex or against the other in a subtle fashion, one not obvious but that will heavily influence the final decision. Is it possible that a mediator can influence the outcome? The answer is yes. A mediator's bias could push a decision one way or another. The subject of bias is complex, and I want to focus on gender issues, as it is a major focus for many individuals when it comes to choosing a mediator.

Bias can be obvious or very subtle. For many reasons, obvious bias is easier to deal with. For starters, it is clearly identifiable. Subtle bias presents more difficulties because it may not even be recognized as such.

Everyone is biased, mediators included. The difference between mediators and the rest of the world is that when working, mediators are not supposed to allow their biases to affect the decision-making process. Any mediator who is conscious of a bias should take care that it does not affect the clients' decision making. Generally, mediators are successful at this, as it is what they are trained to do. If one is conscious of a bias, he or she can neutralize its effect.

It is subtle biases that create fear in divorcing couples. They may fear that a mediator may not be aware of the bias and that it may affect the mediation. Let's take a look at a hypothetical mediator, Ken, who is mediating Daniel and Jean's divorce settlement. They are discussing a custody arrangement, and the parents disagree over the schedule for their three-year-old child, Julie. Daniel wants one alternating week with each parent, while Jean wants a more traditional schedule, with Julie living primarily with her. Let's assume that Ken has a conscious bias in favor of Jean's living schedule. If he is aware of his bias, he may list positive and negative aspects of each plan, brainstorm other available options, give each parent time to explain his or her idea, or quote research studies that equally support or fail to support each parenting plan.

However, let's assume that Ken is not aware of his bias and allows it to influence his work. This bias may show itself in Ken's allowing more time for a discussion of Jean's parenting plan, his quoting research studies to support the daughter's living primarily with Jean, or his illustrating successful plans similar to Jean's or examples of failed parenting plans that sound a lot like Daniel's.

There are actually two closely connected ideas that comprise gender bias. One is a fear that the mediator will side with the same-sex client and win for that client a favorable outcome. The other is a fear that the mediator will side with the opposite-sex client. In the case of our hypothetical mediator, Ken, his subtle gender bias showed that he supported women as primary caregivers, a bias in favor of the opposite sex. If Ken had gender bias in favor of males as primary caregivers, he might propose a plan with the father, Daniel, as the primary caretaker.

During the trainings I conduct for those who want to be mediators, I begin the session on neutrality by saying, "The *appearance* of neutrality is just as important as neutrality. The lack of neutrality is seen as bias." If a client thinks his or her mediator is not being neutral, the perception of bias will destroy the mediation. It is critical that each client perceive the mediator as neutral.

Another new mediator once called me to describe his last meeting with a couple with whom he had difficulty because the case pushed his "bias buttons." It had been an especially difficult case, but he apparently mediated well. At the end of the mediation, the male client said to him, "I thought two or three times that you took Maryann's side, but then I realized that you took my side about two or three times too, so I think that you were fair."

Another mediator described an ongoing case during which, after three sessions, the husband called and said that he thought the mediator was taking his wife's side because of his statements concerning the man's business. The husband was adamantly opposed to having the company appraised, while his wife wanted the appraisal. The mediator told the man that the court would require an appraisal in order to approve the division of assets. The husband felt that this comment showed that the mediator was taking his wife's side. After the phone call, the husband consulted with a lawyer, and it was not until his own lawyer told him that the business had to be valued in order for the judge to approve a final division of their assets that he agreed to the appraisal. The mediator said that the client never offered him an apology, nor did he think the husband changed his mind about the mediator's neutrality. It was a reminder that perception is critical.

In my own practice, at the end of mediation, I ask clients to comment on their experience and, in particular, how it was to have a woman mediator. Men often say something to the effect of "I started off a little concerned that you might favor my wife because you're a woman, but as we went along, I never felt that you took her side." In fact, I've had a number of male clients who added a statement that reflects their gender stereotypes, such as "I don't think it would've been the same with a male mediator. I've gotten upset in here, and that's not something I'd do in front of a man." Some men are uncomfortable with the idea of showing emotions, such as sadness or crying, in front of another man.

The women clients' responses after mediation are more uniform, usually "I know that I wanted a woman, not because she'd take my side, but I was afraid that a man would be biased against me." Women often feel that someone of their own sex will be neutral but that a male mediator will side with their husbands or won't help them. I think the basis of the fear is that women feel more intimidated than men about using the mediation process because it involves negotiations, and women worry that they are not good negotiators. By and large, men feel more secure in their ability to stand up for themselves during a negotiation.

If mediators did not have good communication skills, female mediators would communicate better with their women clients, while male mediators would communicate better with their male clients. Luckily, that is not how mediation works. Mediation skills involve techniques such as active listening, empathy, and reframing that allow the mediator to communicate (which involves listening, understanding, and talking) with each client. In fact, a good mediator can go one step further and actually improve communication between the couple.

However, if mediators are not trained or lack these enhanced communication skills, they are in much the same position as the clients they serve. This means that if your mediator has not had training or does not have the skills of enhanced communication at her fingertips, she will not be able to help you. Then it is probable that the male mediator will communicate better with the male client because he will speak the same language, while the female mediator will communicate better with the female client for the same reason.

You will know if your mediator has good communication skills if each of you feels that the mediator:

- Gives you time to express yourself, and
- Understands what you are saying.

If you each believe both of these statements are true, then the mediator possesses good basic communication skills.

During the introductory session, each of you should have the opportunity to experience both of these basic good communication skills—one reason the introductory session is so important.

I do not think the gender of the mediator makes a difference if you are using a skilled professional. Good mediators communicate equally well with either gender. Their skills allow them to understand and speak in ways that are not limited by gender, but instead allow them to understand what men and women are trying to say and what each really means. As Deborah Tannen wrote in her book *You Just Don't Understand,* "We all want, above all, to be heard—but not merely to be heard. We want to be understood—heard for what we think we are saying, for what we know we meant."

Mediator bias may not be readily apparent. Instead, it may arise during the process, which is why I encourage you to choose a trained and experienced professional with a good reputation. If you are alert to bias, you will most likely feel it during that all-important introductory session. Do not give the mediator the benefit of the doubt; bring it up immediately, and if his or her response isn't adequate, do not choose this mediator. Good mediators do not allow their biases to affect the mediation process; indeed, good mediators carefully select their interventions and their words with vigilant concern for neutrality.

8

Will I Still Need a Lawyer?

The question "Will I still need a lawyer?" may be the most anxiety-ridden one asked of a mediator. Some ask in fear that the answer will be yes, while others fear the opposite. In actual practice, the mediator may respond with an answer that reduces to maybe.

Divorcing couples who choose to use a mediator are often wary of lawyers and do not embrace the idea of consulting one. These couples want a no answer from the mediator. Others, however, want to use a lawyer to review the mediated settlement, a concern voiced more often by women, as well as by those who have considerable assets.

Mediators vary in their attitude toward the involvement of attorneys, ranging from attorney required (the client must consult or retain an independent lawyer) to attorney recommended (the mediator will recommend that the client consult or retain a lawyer) to attorney optional to attorney restricted (the prohibition of outside lawyers during the process).

ATTORNEY REQUIRED

Mediators who require that each client be represented by a separate, independent lawyer are known as attorney-required mediators. This condition is typically clearly stated in the mediation contract. In some contracts, the client must consult with an attorney, while in others, the client must retain an attorney. In this type of mediation practice, each client consults with his and her individual lawyer throughout the process. Typically, the divorcing couple is not allowed to use the same lawyer, as it is considered a conflict of interest for one lawyer to represent two opposing clients.

Mediators who are also lawyers can work with two clients because they do not represent either of them. "Representing" a client means that an attorney is being a zealous advocate of that client and will provide him or her with advice. That's not the job of a mediator. A mediator gives information, not advice. Advice is what someone is told to do concerning the settlement. For example, "You should insist on child support payments until your child is twenty-three." An example of information is "The law in this state mandates child support from birth to age eighteen, and under certain conditions, between ages eighteen and twenty-three."

O. J. Coogler, considered the father of divorce mediation, in his 1978 book *Structured Mediation in Divorce Settlement* described his own procedure, which advocated using one mediator and one consulting attorney, with the divorcing couple consulting the same attorney throughout the mediation process. For a number of good reasons, many in the legal profession were aghast that one attorney would advise individuals who have different interests at stake, and fairly quickly, Coogler's form of mediation fell by the wayside. Lawyers have ethical rules stating that one lawyer should not advise two parties when there is a conflict of interest, and by most everybody's definition, divorcing couples have conflicting interests.

Since Coogler, several modified types of mediation practice

requiring the use of a consulting lawyer have emerged. One type requires each client to have his or her own separate attorney to consult. Retaining an attorney is a condition of the process. Generally, however, the attorneys cannot attend the mediation sessions.

Many mediators who require each client to consult with an independent attorney are not lawyers, and they are concerned that their clients receive the necessary legal information, and they have concerns about their own liability in providing legal information. A growing number of attorney-mediators are also requiring the use of outside lawyers as consultants for similar reasons.

Even if mediators who do require clients to consult with an outside attorney clearly state so in their mediation packet, this is not a guarantee; therefore, it is important for you to ask about this issue prior to engaging a mediator.

ATTORNEY RECOMMENDED

In this type of mediation practice, mediators recommend that each client use the services of an independent, separate attorney, but it is not a requirement. Generally, this recommendation is made during the introductory session, though most include it in their mediation information as well. Mediators in this type of practice fall into two categories: those who recommend the use of an attorney prior to the signing of the final document, and those who recommend consulting an outside attorney throughout the process. In my practice, I recommend that an attorney review the divorce settlement prior to signing, and our packet clearly states this recommendation. In addition, I mention the attorney recommendation during the introductory session and, if possible, during any telephone query.

In this type of practice, it is possible for one spouse to have an attorney and the other to choose not to, though this is not common. Usually, if one spouse consults with an attorney, the other spouse will seek out equal information.

ATTORNEY OPTIONAL

In this form of mediation practice, the use of an attorney is at the client's discretion. Clients who select this mediation form often do not choose to use an independent attorney, perhaps because the mediators may give the impression that they prefer it this way.

As with the attorney-recommended form of practice, the attorney optional allows one spouse to use an outside lawyer, even if the other does not. In both forms, this can create a problem if it is the more powerful of the couple who makes use of an outside lawyer, which puts the mediator in a somewhat difficult position. The situation requires a mediator who is skillful at balancing power differences. This problem, however, has never surfaced in my practice, as it is the less powerful spouse who is most anxious for a lawyer consult.

There are more similarities than differences in these two forms, but it does appear that the attorney-optional form is fading out, while attorney-recommended seems to be gaining in popularity.

ATTORNEY RESTRICTED

In this form of mediation, the use of an outside attorney during the entire mediation process is strongly discouraged, and some mediators actually forbid couples from doing so. The mediator will typically ask prospective clients to sign a contract stating that neither will consult with an independent attorney during the course of their sessions. This restrictive type of mediation practice is not common today and is fast becoming obsolete.

One reason for the emergence of this form was that in the late 1970s and early 1980s, divorce attorneys opposed the practice of mediation and often sabotaged the final mediated settlement. As a way to stop such divorce lawyers from destroying the settlement, mediators would strongly discourage or forbid their clients from using an attorney. However, during the last several years, the attitude of many divorce lawyers has undergone a major shift, and presently there are numerous attorneys who support the mediation process. The primary reason for the death of this type of practice, however, is the liability issue. By preventing a client from consulting with an attorney, mediators may indeed be exposing themselves to the possibility of malpractice, whereas if an attorney is consulted, the responsibility for the advice given lies on his or her shoulders.

As divorce lawyers are more willing to support the mediation process, mediators are more willing for their clients to engage them. However, even today, certainly not all attorneys support mediation, and it is up to you to select one who does.

CONSULTING ATTORNEYS

Over the years, I have had clients who have chosen the most aggressive, adversarial lawyer in the area to be their consulting attorney. In addition to the added cost of such representation, this kind of divorce lawyer creates problems by taking an adversarial stance and filing motions that cause delays, miscommunication, and bad feelings between the spouses. Clients report that it made them feel schizophrenic to have two professionals—the mediator and the attorney—pulling in two opposing directions.

I want to emphasize the danger of choosing such aggressive attorneys, as I witness it with some frequency and see the serious problems it creates. The spouses with aggressive attorneys tend to be those least familiar with mediation and who worry that they will be at a disadvantage in the process. Often, those who are more concerned are women. Their fear is generally encouraged by friends and family and professionals. Many critics, and even friends of mediation, are concerned that women are at a disadvantage at the negotiation table because they are less familiar with financial issues than men.

If you want independent legal input, hire a supportive outside attorney who will be an advocate for you without sabotaging the process. The more your consulting attorney knows about the mediation process, the more helpful she will be.

If you are choosing an attorney-required or -recommended mediator, you will have to have an independent attorney. When you interview a prospective attorney, ask these questions:

1. *Are you supportive of mediation in divorce?* If the response is no, say thank you and leave. If yes, continue with the next question.

2. *Have you worked with a mediator?* If the response is no, I'd be cautious about hiring this attorney. However, if you feel this is someone you could trust and want to pursue retaining her, I would question her understanding of the mediation process. If she responded yes, ask her the names of the mediators with whom she has worked. If she doesn't mention the mediator with whom you are working, I'd bring up the name.

If the attorney has worked with a client in mediation, it's a plus, and if she's worked with the same mediator you've chosen, that's the best possible combination. Otherwise, the client needs to do a lot of explaining to the attorney of how the mediator works.

A way to save yourself a lot of work and the possibility of problems arising is to ask your mediator for a referral. Typically, you'll be provided with a list of attorneys known to be supportive and who have worked with your mediator in the past. My office routinely provides clients with a list of at least three mediation-friendly attorneys from which to choose. Clients are grateful to work with supportive attorneys, and the mediated settlement will not be in danger of being destroyed.

You need to work with an attorney you can talk to, one who listens to you, treats you civilly, and respects you. Many clients do not expect this kind of behavior and are not accorded it. Remember, you are doing the hiring and the paying. Demand good service. And don't hesitate to use your mediator as your guide.

Every person who seeks a divorce in this country must appear in court. Divorce is a legal process, and a judge must approve the settlement. Some people are shocked to find out that couples do not have the right to draft any kind of settlement they choose. Judges want the parties to reach their own reasonable settlement, so it is unusual for a judge to reject a fair agreement, but a judge may reject an unfair agreement even if both parties want it. This is why I don't recommend couples write their own divorce agreement. If the settlement is considered contrary to the applicable law, it may not be approved by the judge, and thus it is crucial to choose a mediator familiar with the judicial practice of the court in your area. After you work to create a settlement, you don't want a judge to reject it. Indeed, as one mediation authority has said, mediation is said to take place "under the shadow of the law."

9

The Final Decision:
Choosing a Mediator

Let's recap what I consider to be the most crucial factors in choosing a mediator:

The Mediator:
- Primary occupation as a mediator
- Experienced
- Private practitioner
- Certified
- Trained
- Appropriate substantive expertise
- Background
- Professional affiliations

Written Materials:
- The mediation packet
- The mediation contract
- The final document

The Practice:
- Fees and payment plans
- Appointment times
- Consulting requirements

THE MEDIATOR

Primary Occupation as a Mediator

The suggestion to use a mediator whose primary job is as a mediator may sound obvious and easily attainable, but it may not be, as full-time mediators are somewhat scarce. A substantial number work primarily in another professional area and mediate part-time. I wouldn't rule out mediators who have a part-time practice, but I'd carefully weigh their responses and consider how much mediation they do.

Experienced

There's little substitute for mediation experience, and I say this knowing that a lot of new mediators will be disheartened. From a client's point of view, experience isn't just an added bonus; depending on the complexity and difficulty of the case, it may be a necessity. Looking back, I realize that some of my early clients might not have had as efficient a mediation process, not because they were impossible people nor because of their complex situation, but because I lacked the experience I have today.

We experienced mediators smile when we reminisce about our early cases. We recognize that experience has sharpened our skills. Though it's true that beginning mediators bring an enthusiasm that is compelling, experience—as long as one is on the right road—makes you better. It could certainly be argued that if one has poor mediation skills, all the experience in the world won't help. But if one is an incompetent mediator, word is apt to get around, and he or she may not be in business very long.

If you have heard good things about a mediator, try that person. On the other hand, if you've heard negative comments, stay away. If you have no information concerning the mediator's reputation, then consider experience. People who have been doing this for several years most likely do it well, or they would be out of business. I can't say with certainty that experience in the field of mediation is more important than experience in any other field, but I do know that mediation involves a combination of skills that improve with practice.

Private Practitioner

This is a confusing topic for some, as a number of people say, "Private versus what? Are there public mediators?" As explained in chapter 5, there are, and they vastly outnumber private mediators. The term *public mediator* generally means that either the individual is a volunteer mediator at a community center or is employed or contracted with a court.

Community centers, usually nonprofits, play a vital role by providing free or low-cost mediation services to community members. A center relies on volunteers who mediate disputes that arise within the community and are then referred by the local court. Generally, community mediators use a specific mediation model, which has several important differences from the traditional divorce mediation model. One is that the mediator is considered a peer, rather than the expert. Peer mediation works exceptionally well in many kinds of cases, but for divorce, a client needs a mediator with expertise in each area of divorce. It is certainly possible that a community mediator has expertise in these areas, and if that is the case, he is appropriate for divorce mediation.

The other kind of public mediator I discussed works for or with the court system. Some states require divorcing couples to see a court mediator if there is a disagreement. This is called mandatory mediation and is generally limited to custody or visitation disputes, and these mediators are extremely well-informed as to those issues. But because these parties work for the court, the facts in your case may not be kept confidential. Also, in some areas, mediators act more as arbitrators and do make decisions. Certainly, a public mediator is better than no mediator at all, but your first step should be to seek the services of a private practitioner

Certified

If you live in a state in which mediators are certified, my advice is to seek such credentials. However, I cannot emphasize how important it is that you consider the certifying body. The best one is an organization of mediators, whether state or local. I predict that in the next few years sundry associations will "certify" mediators. Many local and state bar associations are doing exactly that now. You need to find out not only who is certifying, but what the requirements are.

Remember, certification is a good place to start, but it's a minimal test. It means that the mediators have the basic tools of their profession. If you wonder whether or not your state has certified mediators, don't hesitate to call a mediator and simply ask.

Trained

You must have a trained mediator. Of course, there are some very nice and fair people who might make good mediators, but to help couples work out a divorce settlement, it takes more than just goodwill. People need training in the mediation process. Don't be shy in your inquiries—ask the questions discussed earlier: Who trained you? How long a training program? Was it an Academy of Family Mediators–approved training?

If the mediator is a lawyer, specifically ask if he has had counseling education; if the mediator is a therapist, specifically ask if she had legal courses. Remember, there are three basic areas in mediation: psychological, financial, and legal. Relevant education and training take place within these areas. The forty-hour AFM-approved mediation course is in addition to other professional training. There is no substitute for a mediation training course.

Appropriate Substantive Expertise

Appropriate substantive expertise means appropriate for your situation. You need to determine which areas you need addressed and to choose a mediator who has those qualifications. (Chapter 4 described the possible areas in which you may require your mediator to have a specific expertise.) Review and prioritize your needs. Though it's not easy to determine a mediator's knowledge in an area, once you begin to work with someone, you'll know whether or not she has the expertise you need. If she doesn't, don't hesitate to bring it up if you feel that you are lacking vital information you need in order to make decisions. The mediator may be able to obtain the information herself, you may be referred to a consulting expert, or, as a last result, you may choose to switch mediators.

Background

The men and women who work as private mediators do not share a common history; instead, they come from a variety of backgrounds. A mediator's style typically reflects that individual's professional practice. A majority seem to hail from one of two professional fields, law or psychology. Mediators who are lawyers seem to favor a more legalistic emphasis, while those who are therapists appear to prefer more of a counseling style.

Many people want a one-stop expert mediator service. If this is what you want, you will need a mediator with expertise in all of the areas required for a divorce settlement. This is not as common as one might hope, but these mediators do exist. You just have to do your research.

Whether you use one mediator, a co-mediator partnership, or a team often depends on finances as well as the available mediators in your area. If you are unable to find a mediator who has the characteristics you need you might consider using two mediators, so that between them they have all the expertise you want.

Professional Affiliation

Professional affiliation may be only as important as your state makes it. In most states, only an attorney-mediator can write the actual Divorce Agreement, although in a few states, a nonattorney-mediator may do so.

The final document produced by mediators who are not attorneys is a Memorandum of Understanding, which is not a divorce agreement and is not submitted to a court. An attorney must do that. However, there are mediators who do not have a law license who do write the actual divorce agreement. And indeed, not even all the attorney-mediators do. In other words, do not expect that simply because your mediator has a law license on her wall, she will write the actual divorce agreement. The important point for you to know in advance is the kind of final document your mediator will produce, approximately what it will cost, and whether it can be submitted to the court or if you will need an attorney to turn that document into a legal divorce agreement.

WRITTEN MATERIALS

In addition to assessing the expertise and reputation of the mediator, you will want to take a close look at the written material he or she uses. The mediation packet should provide some idea of that mediator's practice, so be sure to read it thoroughly. The contract (I have included mine on page 118 of Appendix B) should be written clearly and use language you can understand. It should include the following:

- The mediation is voluntary; you can quit at any time.
- The mediator will not make any decisions; the clients make all decisions.
- The mediation will be confidential.
- The mediation fees are clearly stated.
- Each person will fully disclose all assets, liabilities, income, and other relevant financial information.
- The mediator will draft a final document of all agreements.

The mediator should allow adequate time before signing the contract to enable you to have it reviewed by an attorney if you so choose.

THE PRACTICE

Take a good look at the mediation practice. If the information packet doesn't describe cost, ask the approximate cost of the mediation, including the hourly rate and all of the charged services, such as telephone time or document preparation and drafting.

Be certain to ask if there are appointment times that will allow you to conveniently attend the sessions. You will also want to know if there are consulting requirements, for example, with an independent attorney or an accountant. These may be acceptable requirements for you, as long as you are aware and agree to them in advance. It is also wise to get some idea of the cost of these services in advance as well. The more aware you are of the total expense, the better able you'll be to plan financially for the mediation.

· · ·

One of the difficulties in following the steps outlined here is that the need to find a mediator erupts at a crisis time in people's lives. When couples are taking a step toward divorce, their lives are in turmoil. During a crisis, it is certainly difficult to stop and gather information, assess needs, and interview potential mediators, but it is necessary. Remind yourself that the time and energy you invest will be worth it. You will be in a much better position than couples who use an adversarial approach or an incompetent mediator. There's something to be said for doing it the right way.

Countless studies have shown high rates of satisfaction with the mediation process, as well as definite cost savings. It is rare to find someone who regrets using a mediator, unless that mediator was not competent and did a poor job. I hope that this book has provided the information you need to be in a position to avoid such a situation. In divorce, each of you has a lot to lose. Mediation will help each of you win. It is vital that you make sure to choose a good mediator and one that is right for you. Good luck!

Appendix A

Sample Information Packet

DIANE NEUMANN
DIVORCE MEDIATION SERVICES

---

650 Worcester Road   1081 Centre Street
Framingham, MA 01701-5248   Newton, MA 02159
Tel: (508) 879-9095   Tel: (617) 964-7485

Dear Prospective Mediation Client:

Thank you for your interest in **DIANE NEUMANN: DIVORCE MEDIATION SERVICES**. Diane Neumann is a *certified* divorce mediator, certified by the Massachusetts Council on Family Mediation. Enclosed is our Information Packet that explains who we are and the services we offer.

Mediation is a common-sense approach that results in a substantial savings by reducing the cost and stress of divorce. Mediation can help you reach a fair agreement by creating an atmosphere of cooperation that will benefit you and your children.

I am fortunate to have a panel of highly qualified and experienced divorce mediators who consult with me regularly. Each mediator is a licensed Massachusetts attorney and a member of the Massachusetts Council on Family Mediation. They have all taken Divorce Mediation Training, and each has several years of mediation experience.

In addition to Divorce Mediation, I mediate family, business, commercial, and post-divorce disputes, as well as those between unmarried couples and lesbian and gay couples. Please call my office for further information.

As you consider using the mediation process, it would be helpful to share this packet of information with your spouse, partner, or family members. We would be glad to send you additional copies.

A *free* half-hour session is available for clients interested in using Divorce Mediation. The mediator will set aside an optional hour after the Introductory session. You may choose to begin your mediation after the half-hour Introductory session at the mediator's hourly rate, which is quoted in the packet. You will not be charged for this hour if, at that time, you decide not to begin.

If you would like to schedule a *free* Introductory session or speak with a mediator, please call our office at (617) 964-7485 or (508) 879-9095.

Sincerely,

Diane Neumann

DIVORCE MEDIATION
Is It for You?

Do you worry that . . .

- You cannot afford to get divorced?
- The amount of support will be unfair?
- Too much of your money will go to attorneys?
- You cannot communicate with your spouse?
- Your children will suffer?
- You do not know what is fair?
- You need more knowledge concerning finances?
- You won't get accurate legal information?
- Tax consequences will not be considered?
- You will end up with a court battle?
- It is going to get worse?

If you answer yes to one or more of these questions, mediation is for you. Mediation has been found to help in every one of these areas. In fact, studies show that divorce mediation results in (1) increased personal adjustment, (2) significant financial savings, and (3) emotionally healthier children.

DIANE NEUMANN:
DIVORCE MEDIATION SERVICES
Information Packet

A MEDIATED DIVORCE

In the United States today, more than half of all marriages end in divorce. Often the divorce process itself is traumatic, bitter, and expensive. The adversarial setting for divorce intensifies the hostility and winner-take-all attitude. A fairer, more civilized way to reach a separation or a divorce settlement is through mediation.

The following is a direct quote from the report of the Massachusetts Special Commission on Probate and Family Court Procedures:

> The evidence to date suggests that mediated settlements in marital disputes simply last longer and work better than adjudicated settlements because the parties who helped craft the settlements have a greater stake in making them work.

Mediation is a way for separating and divorcing men and women to reach fair settlements. Our professional mediators will ensure that every divorce issue is addressed and resolved in order for you to obtain a divorce in the Commonwealth of Massachusetts.

Clients from out of state may also use our mediation services; please call the office for specific information.

FINANCIAL DISCLOSURE

All financial information must be documented prior to the final Separation Agreement, a process known as legal discovery. The divorce court requires discovery, and at the end of mediation, you will be prepared for court.

CONFIDENTIALITY

Under Massachusetts General Laws, legal privilege has been extended to divorce mediators. Under this law, all mediation sessions are confidential. Neither the mediator nor any notes nor mediation documents may be subpoenaed into court. You will be asked to sign a mediation contract agreeing to the confidentiality of the mediation.

DIVORCE MEDIATION SESSIONS

You may use mediation at any point before, during, or after your separation or divorce. Mediation is an open process, and you may consult with a professional of your choice at any time during the process. If there are minor children (under age eighteen), the average mediation consists of five sessions. The average length of each session is 1½ to 2 hours. A typical mediation sequence follows:

Introductory Meeting—A Free Half-Hour Session:
> The mediator will describe mediation, provide you with a negotiating framework for your settlement, and answer your questions.

Billable time begins with the one-hour optional time slot scheduled for you, which immediately follows the Introductory Meeting.

Child Custody:
> This session defines and discusses legal and physical custody of your child, and includes a parenting plan appropriate for Probate Court.

Child Support:
> This meeting concerns income, expenses as well as the actual work-up of the Massachusetts Child Support Guidelines Worksheet, an overview of present and future legal child support issues, and college expenses.

Property Division:
> The division of assets typically begins with an in-depth look at the marital house, and includes tax consequences at present and future transfer and sale, and financial and tax implications of sole or continued joint ownership.

Asset and Liability Division:

A continuation of property division, including pension plans, employee plans, savings accounts, stocks and bonds, vehicles, business valuations, and house contents. Liability decisions include responsibility for mortgage, equity lines, car loans, promissory notes, life insurance and pension loans, credit card debt, and all other debt.

Insurance Benefits and Divorce Process:

This session covers medical, dental, life, and disability insurance and responsibility for uninsured expenses, child tax exemptions, tax filings, and additional issues required due to your particular situation.

At the end of the Mediation sessions, you each will receive a written copy of your settlement, called the Separation Agreement (also known as the Divorce Agreement). **In Massachusetts, you may file directly for your own divorce.** The mediator will assist you in your own filing, or you each may have an attorney represent you.

COMPREHENSIVE DIVORCE MEDIATION SERVICES

All of the following areas are included in our comprehensive divorce agreements:

- Child Custody
- Child Support
- College Expenses
- Property and Liability Division
- Alimony

- Medical and Dental Insurance and Costs
- Tax Deductions
- Tax Filings
- Capital-Gain Tax Consequences

THE PANEL OF MEDIATORS

Divorce Mediation Services is unique in that we offer you a choice of mediators. Every mediator on the panel is a licensed Massachusetts attorney trained in basic and advanced divorce mediation by Divorce Mediation Training Associates. All of the mediators are members of the Massachusetts Bar Association Family Law Section and the Massachusetts Council on Family Mediation, a state organization requiring mediators to maintain certain professional and ethical standards. Diane Neumann consults regularly with each mediator.

All of the mediators at *Divorce Mediation Services* offer comprehensive divorce mediation. Depending on the time you prefer to schedule appointments, you may choose among the following four highly qualified and experienced mediators:

- Susan Sprague Walters
- Laurie S. Udell
- Mary T. Johnston
- Roger Dupont

OTHER MEDIATION SERVICES

In addition to Comprehensive Divorce Agreements, Diane Neumann also offers all of the following types of mediation:

- Post-Divorce
- Unmarried Couples (Paternity)
- Business and Commercial
- Lesbian/Gay Couples
- Family
- Premarital

Sample Mediation Contract

Please read this contract and be prepared to sign it at your next mediation session. You may consult with an attorney prior to signing this contract.

MEDIATION CONTRACT

We are requesting services from Diane Neumann of Divorce Mediation Services, under the following conditions:

1. This mediation is voluntary. Either of us may choose to end it at any time.

2. We will make all of the decisions; the mediator cannot impose any decision upon us.

3. We will each fully disclose and document all of our financial income, assets, and liabilities during the mediation. We may each use professionals as advisors, but each of us accepts full responsibility for the reasonable accuracy of these figures.

4. Mediation sessions are totally confidential. We will not subpoena the mediator nor his/her files in any legal proceeding.

5. Either of us may seek professional and/or legal advice at any time during the mediation. The mediator recommends that

we each have a separate, independent attorney review our Separation Agreement before signing it.

6. The mediator will not disclose any information concerning us to a third party without prior consent.

7. We each consent to our mediator's contacting our respective lawyers or counselors at any time or to respond to such contact, and to release any information relevant to that professional's client only.

8. At the conclusion of the sessions, the mediator will prepare a written Separation Agreement, setting forth our agreements. We each will receive a copy.

9. Each of us understands that the mediator is not acting as an attorney and is not representing either or both of us.

MEDIATION FEES

1. The mediation fee is $240 per hour.* Preparation of written documents are billed at the same hourly rate. Typical documents prepared by the mediator are the Memorandum, the court Separation Agreement (the actual Divorce Agreement), and the court Affidavit.

All other services are billed at the same hourly rate and include:
a. Document drafting and review,
b. Telephone time.

2. Mediation services are based on an hourly fee. You may choose to pay fees in one of two options:

a. A ten-hour retainer, which will be applied toward mediation costs. All unused funds from the retainer will be returned.

---

*This hourly fee will apply for twelve months from the date of the signing of the Mediation Contract, at which time the hourly fee may be adjusted.

b. A payment plan. The full payment for each session is due at the end of that session.

3. We accept the following forms of payment:
   a. personal check,
   b. bank cards; VISA and MasterCard only,
   c. bank checks, money orders, and cash.

4. Outstanding balances that are not paid within thirty days after services are rendered will incur a late charge or 10 percent of the outstanding balance for each month the balance remains overdue. A retainer will be required for future mediation services.

5. You must provide a two-working day (48-hour) notice (M–F, excluding holidays) to cancel or change a mediation session. You will be charged the full fee for missed appointments or late notice.

6. Each of us is responsible for his/her individual mediation charges and one-half of all mediation charges unless agreed otherwise.

_____   _____
Wife's Signature   Date

_____   _____
Husband's Signature   Date

_____   _____
Mediator's Signature   Date

Academy of Family Mediators Standards of Practice for Family and Divorce Mediation

Preamble

Mediation is a family-centered conflict resolution process in which an impartial third party assists the participants to negotiate a consensual and informed settlement. In mediation, whether private or public, decision-making authority rests with the parties. The role of the mediator includes reducing the obstacles to communication, maximizing the exploration of alternatives, and addressing the needs of those it is agreed are involved or affected.

Mediation is based on principles of problem solving that focus on the needs and interests of the participants; fairness; privacy; self-determination; and the best interest of all family members.

These standards are intended to assist and guide public, private, voluntary, and mandatory mediation. It is understood that the manner of implementation and mediator adherence to these standards may be influenced by local law or court rule.

Initiating the Process

Definition and Description of Mediation

The mediator shall define mediation and describe the differences and similarities between mediation and other procedures for dispute resolution. In defining the process, the mediator shall delineate it from therapy, counseling, custody evaluation, arbitration, and advocacy.

Identification of Issues

The mediation shall elicit sufficient information from the participants so that they can mutually define and agree on the issues to be resolved in mediation.

Appropriateness of Mediation

The mediator shall help the participants evaluate the benefits, risks, and costs of mediation and the alternatives available to them.

Mediator's Duty of Disclosure

Biases. The mediator shall disclose to the participants any biases or strong views relating to the issues to be mediated.

Training and Experience. The mediator's education, training, and experience to mediate the issues should be accurately described to the participants.

Procedures

The mediator shall reach an understanding with the participants regarding the procedures to be followed in mediation. This includes but is not limited to the practice as to separate meetings between a participant and the mediator, confidentiality, use of legal services, the involvement of additional parties, and conditions under which mediation may be terminated.

Mutual Duties and Responsibilities

The mediator and the participants shall agree upon the duties and responsibilities that each is accepting in the mediation process. This may be a written or verbal agreement.

Impartiality and Neutrality

Impartiality

The mediator is obligated to maintain impartiality toward all participants. Impartiality means freedom from favoritism or bias, either in word or action. Impartiality implies a commitment to aid all participants, as opposed to a single individual, in reaching a mutually satisfactory agreement. Impartiality means that a mediator will not play an adversarial role.

The mediator has a responsibility to maintain impartiality while raising questions for the parties to consider as to the fairness, equity, and feasibility of proposed options for settlement.

Neutrality

Neutrality refers to the relationship that the mediator has with the disputing parties. If the mediator feels, or any one of the participants states, that the mediator's background or personal experiences would prejudice the mediator's performance, the mediator should withdraw from mediation unless all agree to proceed.

Prior Relationships

A mediator's actual or perceived impartiality may be compromised by social or professional relationships with one of the participants at any point in time. The mediator shall not proceed if previous legal or counseling services have been provided to one of the participants. If such services have been provided to both participants, mediation shall not proceed unless the prior relationship has been discussed, the role of the mediator made distinct from the earlier relationship, and the participants given the opportunity to freely choose to proceed.

Relationship to Participants

The mediator should be aware that post-mediation professional or social relationships may compromise the mediator's continued availability as a neutral third party.

Conflict of Interest

A mediator should disclose any circumstances to the participants that might cause a conflict of interest.

Costs and Fees

Explanation of Fees

The mediator shall explain the fees to be charged for mediation and any related costs and shall agree with the participants on how the fees will be shared and the manner of payment.

Reasonable Fees

When setting fees, the mediator shall ensure that they are explicit, fair, reasonable, and commensurate with the service to be performed. Unearned fees should be promptly returned to the clients.

Contingent Fees

It is inappropriate for a mediator to charge contingent fees or to base fees on the outcome of mediation.

Referrals and Commissions

No commissions, rebates, or similar forms of remuneration shall be given or received for referral of clients for mediation services.

Confidentiality and Exchange of Information

Confidentiality

Confidentiality relates to the full and open disclosure necessary for the mediation process. A mediator shall foster the confidentiality of the process.

Limits of Confidentiality

The mediator shall inform the parties at the initial meeting of limitations on confidentiality, such as statutorily or judicially mandated reporting.

Appearing in Court. The mediator shall inform the parties of circumstances under which mediators may be compelled to testify in court.

Consequences of Disclosure of Facts Between Parties. The mediator shall discuss with the participants the potential consequences of their disclosure of facts to each other during the mediation process.

Release of Information

The mediator shall obtain the consent of the participants prior to releasing information to others. The mediator shall maintain confidentiality and render anonymous all identifying information when materials are used for research or training purposes.

Caucus

The mediator shall discuss policy regarding confidentiality for individual caucuses. In the event that a mediator, on consent of the participants, speaks privately with any person not represented in mediation, including children, the mediator shall define how information received will be used.

Storage and Disposal of Records

The mediator shall maintain confidentiality in the storage and disposal of records.

Full Disclosure

The mediator shall require disclosure of all relevant information in the mediation process, as would reasonably occur in the judicial discovery process.

Self-Determination

Responsibilities of the Participants and the Mediator

The primary responsibility for the resolution of a dispute rests with the participants. The mediator's obligation is to assist the disputants in reaching an informed and voluntary settlement. At no time shall a mediator coerce a participant into agreement or make a substantive decision for any participant.

Responsibility to Third Parties

The mediator has a responsibility to promote the participants' consideration of the interests of children and other persons affected by the agreement. The mediator also has a duty to assist parents to examine, apart from their own desires, the separate and individual needs of such people. The participants shall be encouraged to seek outside professional consultation when appropriate or when they are otherwise unable to agree on the needs of any individual affected by the agreement.

Professional Advice

Independent Advice and Information

The mediator shall encourage and assist the participants to obtain independent expert information and advice when such information is needed to reach an informed agreement or to protect the rights of a participant.

Providing Information

A mediator shall give information only in those areas where qualified by training or experience.

Independent Legal Counsel

When the mediation may affect legal rights or obligations, the mediator shall advise the participants to seek independent legal counsel prior to resolving the issues and in conjunction with formalizing an agreement.

Parties' Ability to Negotiate

The mediator shall ensure that each participant has had an opportunity to understand the implications and ramifications of available options. In the event a participant needs either additional information or assistance in order for the negotiations to proceed in a fair and orderly manner or for an agreement to be reached, the mediator shall refer the individual to appropriate resources.

Procedural Factors

The mediator has a duty to ensure balanced negotiations and should not permit manipulative or intimidating negotiation techniques.

Psychological Factors

The mediator shall explore whether the participants are capable of participating in informed negotiations. The mediator may postpone mediation and refer the parties to appropriate resources if necessary.

Concluding Mediation

Full Agreement

The mediator shall discuss with the participants the process for formalization and implementation of the agreement.

Partial Agreement

When the participants reach a partial agreement, the mediator shall discuss with them procedures available to resolve the remaining issues.

Without Agreement

Termination by Participants. The mediator shall inform the participants of their right to withdraw from mediation at any time and for any reason.

Termination by Mediator. If the mediator believes that participants are unable or unwilling to participate meaningfully in the process or that a reasonable agreement is unlikely, the mediator may suspend or terminate mediation and should encourage the parties to seek appropriate professional help.

Impasse. If the participants reach a final impasse, the mediator should not prolong unproductive discussions that would result in emotional and monetary costs to the participants.

Training and Education

Training

A mediator shall acquire substantive knowledge and procedural skill in the specialized area of practice. This may include but is not limited to family and human development, family law, divorce procedures, family finances, community resources, the mediation process, and professional ethics.

Continuing Education

A mediator shall participate in continuing education and be personally responsible for ongoing professional growth. A mediator is encouraged to join with other mediators and members of related professions to promote mutual professional development.

Advertising

A mediator shall make only accurate statements about the mediation process, its costs and benefits, and the mediator's qualifications.

The Responsibility of the Mediator Toward Other Mediators

Relationship with Other Mediators

A mediator should not mediate any dispute that is being mediated by another mediator without first endeavoring to consult with the person or persons conducting the mediation.

Co-mediation

In those situations where more than one mediator is participating in a particular case, each mediator has a responsibility to keep the others informed of developments essential to a cooperative effort.

Relationships with Other Professionals

A mediator should respect the complementary relationship between mediation and legal, mental health, and other social services and should promote cooperation with other professionals.

Advancement of Mediation

Mediation Service

A mediator is encouraged to provide some mediation service in the community for nominal or no fee.

Promotion of Mediation

A mediator shall promote the advancement of mediation by encouraging and participating in research, publishing, or other forms of professional and public education.

Participating Organizations

Academy of Family Mediators
American Academy of
  Matrimonial Lawyers
American Arbitration
  Association
American Association for
  Mediated Divorce
American Association of
  Pastoral Counselors
American Bar Association—
Family Law Section,
Mediation and
Arbitration Committee
Special Committee on
Alternative Dispute
Resolution
American Psychological
  Association
Association of Family and
  Conciliation Courts

Association of Family and Conciliation Courts— California Chapter

British Columbia Judges Committee on Family Law

California State Bar, Family Law Section, Custody and Visitation Committee

Canadian Federal Government— Department of Justice

Children's Judicial Resource Council

Colorado Bar, Family Law Section

Council on Accreditation of Services for Families and Children

Family Mediation Association

Family Mediation Center, Scottsdale, Arizona

Family Mediation Service of Ontario

Hennepin County Court Services

Legal Aid of Quebec

Los Angeles Conciliation Court

Maricopa County Conciliation Court

Mediation Association of Southern Arizona

Mediation Consortium of Washington State

Mediation Council of Illinois

Mediation Institute of California

Minnesota Council of Family Mediation

Montreal Conciliation Court

National Association of Social Workers

National Council on Family Relations

National Institute for Dispute Resolution

Northwest Mediation Service

Ontario Association for Family Mediation

Pima County Superior Court

Pinal County Conciliation Court

San Diego County Superior Court Family Services

Society of Professionals in Dispute Resolution

South Florida Council on Divorce Mediation

Southern California Mediation Network

State Bar of California— Legal Specialization Committee

Wisconsin Association of Family and Divorce Mediators

Practitioner Members of the Academy of Family Mediators (AFM)*

ALABAMA

Borden, Lee
Alabama Divorce Mediation
3280 Morgan Dr.
Birmingham, AL 35216
(205) 979-6960, voice
(205) 979-6902, fax

Kok, Sammye Oden, JD
Dominick Fletcher Yeilding
Wood & Lloyd, PA†
2121 Highland Ave.
Birmingham, AL 35205
(205) 939-0033, voice
(205) 933-6133, fax

Kramer, Luther E., MDiv
219 Grove Ave.
Huntsville, AL 35801
(205) 534-2560, voice
(205) 536-5508, fax

ALASKA

Anderson, Kathleen G.
Arbitration and Mediation Group
P.O. Box 240783
Anchorage, AK 99524
(907) 345-3801, voice
(907) 345-0006, fax

Dearborn, Mary Ann
Dearborn Family Mediation
308 G Street, #202
Anchorage, AK 99501
(907) 276-6001, voice

*This list is as of 1996. For more up-to-date information, call the AFM at 1-800-292-4AFM.
†Professional Association

Jackinsky, Sara Louise, MS
Peninsula Mediation
Box 1044
Homer, AK 99603
(907) 235-6417, voice
(907) 235-1045, fax

Peterson, Drew, JD
Family and General Mediator
4325 Laurel, #235
Anchorage, AK 99508
(907) 561-1518, voice
(907) 562-0780, fax

Sullivan-Batra, Lorraine
27345 Golden Eagle Dr.
Chugiak, AK 99567
(907) 279-3695, voice
(907) 258-2157, fax

ARIZONA

Arriola, Shannon R.
Arriola, Silver & Assoc.
10900 N. Scottsdale Rd., Suite 201
Scottsdale, AZ 85254
(602) 596-1226, voice
(602) 948-8163, fax

Borum, Joy B., JD
7520 E. 2nd St., #3
Scottsdale, AZ 85251
(602) 945-8909, voice
(602) 941-2650, fax

Capra, Shari M.
340 E. Palm Lane, Suite 275
Phoenix, AZ 85004
(602) 271-4244, voice
(602) 271-9308, fax

Crabb, Jimmy
3010 E. Loretta Dr.
Tucson, AZ 85716-2527
(602) 323-1801, voice
(602) 323-1801, fax

Cramer, Clarence, MA
Conciliation Court Pinal County
119 W. Central Ave.
Coolidge, AZ 85228
(520) 723-3077, voice
(520) 868-7354, fax

Dalton, Jefferson R.
Gila County Superior Court
1400 Ash St.
Globe, AZ 85501
(602) 425-3231, x270, voice
(602) 425-7802, fax

Dashiell, Jeannine P., MA
5040 N. 15th Ave.
Phoenix, AZ 85015
(602) 870-0053, voice

Devoy, Linda, JD
Accord Mediation Services
177 N. Church Ave., Suite 200
Tucson, AZ 85701-1117
(602) 628-7777, voice
(602) 623-5074, fax

Giles, Gordon B., Esq.
Divorce Mediation Center
7520 E. 2nd St., Suite 7
Scottsdale, AZ 85251
(602) 994-8787, voice
(602) 941-2650, fax

Gourley, Ruth L., MC
1703 S. Cholla Ave.
Mesa, AZ 85202
(602) 506-2300, voice
(602) 506-2029, fax

Hawkins, Grace M., ACSW, CISW
Family Center of Conciliation
   Court
32 N. Stone Ave., #1704
Tucson, AZ 85701
(602) 740-5590, voice
(602) 624-4034, fax

Infeld, Kathleen D., MS, RN
Scottsdale Counseling &
   Mediation Assoc.
10900 N. Scottsdale Rd., Suite
   201
Scottsdale, AZ 85254
(602) 948-2635, voice
(602) 948-8163, fax

Joy, Marlene, PhD
Scottsdale Counseling &
   Mediation Assoc.
10900 N. Scottsdale Rd., #201
Scottsdale, AZ 85254
(602) 948-2635, voice
(602) 948-8163, fax

Kaminsky, Harry, ACSW
Regional Vice President
American Arbitration Association
333 E. Osborn Rd., Suite 310
Phoenix, AZ 85012
(602) 234-0950, voice
(602) 230-2151, fax

Kelty, Sharon F.
Conciliation Services of Pinal
   County
119 W. Central
Coolidge, AZ 85228
(520) 723-3077, voice
(520) 868-7354, fax

Kersey, Fred L., PhD
Pima County Conciliation Court
32 N. Stone Ave., #1704
Tucson, AZ 85701
(520) 740-5590, voice
(520) 624-4034, fax

Lane, Pamela S.
8636 E. Jumping Cholla Circle
Gold Canyon, AZ 85219
(602) 982-1388, voice

LaVelle, Margaret E., MEd
4524 N. 13th Ave.
Phoenix, AZ 85013
(602) 264-7601, voice

Lee, S. Terry, JD
Gillespie & Associates
10220 N. 31st Ave., Suite 225
Phoenix, AZ 85051
602-870-9700, voice
602-870-9783, fax

Moore, John P.
394 N. 3rd Ave.
Phoenix, AZ 85003
(602) 258-3400, voice
(602) 258-7557, fax

Musty, Timothy A., MSSW, CISW
2200 E. River Rd., Suite 118A
Tucson, AZ 85718-6579
(520) 577-0079, voice
(520) 577-0169, fax

Nicholson, Ford T.
3912 S. Lone Palm Dr.
Tucson, AZ 85730
(602) 740-5590, voice
(602) 624-4034, fax

Norbeck, Suzanna Anstine
Divorce & Family Mediation
1807 E. Hale
Mesa, AZ 85203
(602) 649-9970, voice

Orman, Betty, MSW, ACSW, CISW
5262 N. Adobe Circle
Tucson, AZ 85750
(520) 795-0300, voice
(520) 747-3912, fax

Quattrocchi, Allison H., JD
Family Mediation Center
7520 E. 2nd St., #3
Scottsdale, AZ 85251
(602) 949-9511, voice
(602) 941-2650, fax

Remers, Ann Jordan, JD
Attorney at Law
5022 E. Calle Guebabi
Tucson, AZ 85718
(502) 529-8610, voice
(502) 529-8610, fax

Richter, Kay, MSW, JD
5760 Mina Vista
Tucson, AZ 85718
(602) 577-5275, voice

Schoeneman, Russell, PhD
Maricopa County Conciliation
   Services
201 W. Jefferson
Phoenix, AZ 85003
(602) 506-3298, voice
(602) 506-7867, fax

Tobin, Joan F.
2171 E. La Donna Dr.
Tempe, AZ 85283
(602) 839-8992, voice

Topp, Lynda K.
Pima County Conciliation Court
32 N. Stone Ave., #1704
Tucson, AZ 85701
(602) 740-5590, voice
(602) 624-4034, fax

Yandell, Karen
1357 E. Chilton Dr.
Tempe, AZ 85283
(602) 506-3296, voice

CALIFORNIA

Adams, Nancy A., MA, MFCC
550 N. State St., Suite 4
Ukiah, CA 95482
(707) 468-7871, voice
(707) 467-0121, fax

Allen, Elizabeth L.
Coast to Coast Mediation Center
4401 Manchester Ave., Suite 202
Encinitas, CA 92024
(619) 436-8414, voice
(619) 436-7943, fax

Allen, Janet W.
Pacific Mediation Services
2223 Avenida De La Playa, #212
La Jolla, CA 92037
(619) 459-4110, voice

Angel-Levy, Penny, MFCC
5060 Shoreham Pl., Suite 200
San Diego, CA 92122
(619) 458-5878, voice

Baker-Jackson, Maxine, JD,
    LSCW, RN
7504 Via Lorado
Rancho Palos Verdes, CA 90275
(310) 377-5311, voice

Cameron, Ronald L.
Dispute Resolution Center
2100 Goodyear Ave., Suite 11
Ventura, CA 93003
(805) 985-1967, voice
(805) 985-2449, fax

Cartier, Richard M., JD
P.O. Box 16368
Fresno, CA 93755-6368
(209) 439-7606, voice
(209) 225-4322, fax

Cloke, Kenneth
Center for Dispute Resolution
2411 18th St.
Santa Monica, CA 90405
(310) 399-4426, voice
(310) 399-5906, fax

Cogen, Michael J., JD, PhD
Wood Island
60 E. Sir Francis Drake Blvd.,
    Suite 210
Larkspur, CA 94925
(415) 925-9760, voice
(415) 461-8038, fax

Cohen, Lester
Law and Mediation Offices
    of Lester Cohen
707 Broadway, Suite 1100
San Diego, CA 92101
(619) 595-1566, voice
(619) 232-2704, fax

Dale, Margaret A.
P.O. Box 770
Sonoma, CA 95476
(707) 938-0523, voice
(707) 539-6555, fax

Daly, Bonnie R.
701 Kettner Blvd., #101
San Diego, CA 92101
(619) 696-9644, voice

Delzer, Carol, MFCC, MA
Carol Delzer—Law and
  Mediation
5650 Sunrise Blvd., Suite 5
Citrus Heights, CA 95610
(916) 967-5555, voice
(916) 863-2300, fax

Eddy, William A., LCSW, JD
Attorney and Mediator
160 Thorn St., Suite 2
San Diego, CA 92103-5691
(619) 291-9644, voice
(619) 692-4061, fax

Esbenshade, Alice Houghton
226 E. Canon Perdido, #1
Santa Barbara, CA 93101
(805) 966-1212, voice
(805) 966-1212, fax

Folberg, Jay, JD
University of San Francisco
  School of Law's Dean's Office
Ignatian Heights
San Francisco, CA 94117
(415) 666-6307, voice

Foster, Nancy J., JD
Northern California Mediation
  Center
100 Tamal Plaza, Suite 175
Corte Madera, CA 94925
(415) 927-1422, voice
(415) 927-1477, fax

Gallaway, Mary Ann, MA
650 Howe Ave., Suite 730
Sacramento, CA 95825
(916) 487-6949, voice
(916) 924-1699, fax

Gefis, Carol G.
LegalEase Mediation & Legal
  Services
600 City Parkway W., Suite 230
Orange, CA 92668
(714) 748-0100, voice
(714) 385-8011, fax

Goldman, Judith Roth, MA,
  MFCC
270–26th St., #206
Santa Monica, CA 90402
(310) 394-2501, voice
(310) 392-5089, fax

Greenberg, Genell G., MSW
Law & Mediation Offices of
  Genell G. Greenberg
Plaza Del Mar
12526 High Bluff Dr., Suite 290
San Diego, CA 92130
(619) 792-3550, voice
(619) 792-3890, fax

Greenwald, Lynn M., MA
1100 Glendon Ave., #1510
Los Angeles, CA 90024
(310) 208-7406, voice
(818) 789-0690, fax

Hughes, Marilyn J., MA, MFCC
1121 W. Vine, #12A
Lodi, CA 95240
(209) 368-0971, voice
(209) 368-5546, fax

Hurvitz, Yardenna, JD
433 N. Camden Dr., 12th Fl.
Beverly Hills, CA 90210
(310) 205-2056, voice
(310) 205-2057, fax

Hyde, Heather, JD
501 Stockton Ave.
San Jose, CA 95126
(408) 995-6425, voice
(408) 995-6427, fax

Jansen, Faith
Attorney at Law
200 Gregory Lane, Suite B-2
Pleasant Hill, CA 94523
(510) 671-9200, voice
(510) 827-2116, fax

Jantz, Vivian
Meridian Mediation
P.O. Box 1485
Jamestown, CA 95327
(209) 984-5594, voice
(209) 984-0628, fax

Jordan, Althea Lee
Jordan & Miller
Attorneys at Law
385 Sherman Ave., #1
Palo Alto, CA 94306
(415) 325-8800, voice
(415) 325-8837, fax

Kachorek, John, PhD
220 Second St.
Encinitas, CA 92024
(619) 942-3194, voice

Keller, David B.
Keller Consultants
11963 Caneridge Rd.
San Diego, CA 92128
(619) 658-7487, voice

Kelly, Joan B., PhD
Northern California Mediation
  Center
100 Tamal Plaza, Suite 175
Corte Madera, CA 94925
(415) 927-1422, voice
(415) 927-1477, fax

Kresge, Jennifer
P.O. Box 405
1308 Main St., Suite 114
St. Helena, CA 94574
(707) 963-5586, voice

Lebental, Carole E., LCSW, BCD
23717 Hawthorne Blvd.,
  Suite 102
Torrance, CA 90505
(310) 517-7990, voice
(310) 373-1654, fax

Lemmon, John, PhD
Lemmon Mediation Institute
5248 Boyd Ave.
Oakland, CA 94618
(510) 547-8089, voice

Levitt, Howard
1305 Woodlow Court
Westlake Village, CA 91361
(310) 205-2056, voice
(310) 205-2057, fax

Lund, Mary, PhD
2510 Main St., #201
Santa Monica, CA 90405
(310) 392-6163, voice

Luvaas, Jon, JD
Mediation Law Office
341 Broadway
P.O. Box 3276
Chico, CA 95927
(916) 343-4934, voice
(916) 899-7634, fax

Lyster, Mimi E.
Center for Settlement Services,
    Inc.
P.O. Box 3034
Mammoth Lakes, CA 93546
(619) 934-7539, voice
(619) 934-9539, fax

McAdams, Hedy
467 Hamilton Ave., #8
Palo Alto, C A 94301
(415) 325-3371, voice

McDonald, Brian
Spolter, McDonald, & Mannion
Pier 9
San Francisco, CA 94111
(415) 956-0211, voice

McGough, David
The Mediation Center of Walnut
    Creek
1281 Boulevard Way, Suite A
Walnut Creek, CA 94595
(510) 934-4680, voice
(510) 934-2001, fax

McGough, Ruth Dickerson
The Mediation Center of Walnut
    Creek
1281 Boulevard Way, Suite A
Walnut Creek, CA 94595
(510) 934-4680, voice
(510) 934-2001, fax

McInaney, Michele G.
Law and Mediation
540 Bird Ave.
San Jose, CA 95125
(408) 279-1481, voice
(408) 292-7181, fax

Meierding, Nina R., MS, JD
Mediation Center for Family Law
857 E. Main St.
Ventura, CA 93001
(805) 643-3543, voice
(805) 653-6107, fax

Mellor, Dean J.
1337 Ocean Ave.
Santa Monica, CA 90401
(310) 451-1004, voice

Millen, Richard H.
Side by Side Divorce Service
15235 Valley Vista Blvd.
Sherman Oaks, CA 91403
(818) 501-2787, voice
(818) 501-2787, fax

Moes, Lacy N., Esq.
735 State St., Suite 633
Santa Barbara, CA 93101
(805) 966-7844, voice
(805) 963-9140, fax

Newman, Michael
539 Hartnell
Monterey, CA 93940
(408) 649-0957, voice
(408) 649-0702, fax

Penn, Stephen W.
Attorney at Law
16360 Monterey Rd., Suite 120
Morgan Hill, CA 95037
(408) 776-1525, voice
(408) 778-5447, fax

Peterson, Sharon Shields, JD
Attorney at Law
2067 1st Ave.
San Diego, CA 92101
(619) 234-1388, voice
(619) 531-0166, fax

Rempel, Susan C., PhD
433 N. Camden Dr., Suite 400
Beverly Hills, CA 90210
(310) 858-6820, voice
(818) 952-3241, fax

Rose, Chip
4340 Scotts Valley Dr., Suite J
Scotts Valley, CA 95066-4541
(408) 438-1604, voice
(408) 439-0703, fax

Rosenberg, Steven
591 Redwood Hwy., Suite 2275
Mill Valley, CA 94941
(415) 383-5544, voice
(415) 381-4301, fax

Rouin, Carole C.
Center for Divorce Mediation
One World Trade Center,
  Suite 2320
Long Beach, CA 90831-2320
(310) 437-5409, voice
(310) 437-4610, fax

Ruth-Heffelbower, Duane, JD,
  MDiv
Mediation Associates/Center for
  Peacemaking and Conflict
  Studies
1450 Tollhouse Rd., Suite 105
Clovis, CA 93611
(209) 323-4579, voice
(209) 323-4579, fax

Samis, Michelle
Child Custody Mediation
3065 Porter St., Suite 102
Soquel, CA 95073
(408) 475-3661, voice

Saposnek, Donald T., PhD
Family Mediation Service
6233 Soquel Dr., Suite E
Aptos, CA 95003
(408) 476-9225, voice
(408) 662-9056, fax

Scherman, Susan A.
Attorney at Law/Mediator
465 California St., #200
San Francisco, CA 94104
(415) 989-8999, voice
(415) 989-8947, fax

Schiff, Patsy K., JD
Attorney & Mediator
1409 28th St., #210
Sacramento, CA 95816-6404
(916) 442-5518, voice
(916) 442-3866, fax

Scott, Michael, LMFCC
Family Mediation Service
333 Church St., Suite B
Santa Cruz, CA 95060
(408) 423-0521, voice

Shawn, Joel
California Mediation Service
1388 Sutter St., #1210
San Francisco, CA 94109
(415) 567-7000, voice
(415) 567-6116, fax

Silverman, Bruce S., JD
Laughlin Falbo Levy & Moresi
2 Embarcadero Center, Suite 500
San Francisco, CA 94111-3823
(415) 781-6676, x332, voice
(415) 781-6823, fax

Sofaer, Pearl
SOFAIR Mediation
1824 Chestnut St.
Redding, CA 96001
(916) 225-5707, voice
(916) 245-6337, fax

Stevens, Jan, MA
Divorce Alternatives
5811 Amaya Dr., #203
La Mesa, CA 91942
(619) 589-9333, voice
(619) 698-8887, fax

Stewart, Jay, MA
P.O. Box 2004
Petaluma, CA 94953
(707) 763-0918, voice
(707) 763-0978, fax

Strachan, Angus, PhD
Divorce and Family Therapy
  Specialists
2510 Main St., Suite 201
Santa Monica, CA 90405
(310) 392-2293, voice
(310) 392-6043, fax

Thomas, Dianne, MA
325 Avila Rd.
San Mateo, CA 94402
(415) 349-0461, voice
(415) 358-9666, fax

Throgmorton, Jamie J.
Hammer, Jacobs, &
  Throgmorton
Ten Almaden Blvd., 10th Fl.
San Jose, CA 95113-2237
(408) 297-8400, voice
(408) 297-8488, fax

Walters, Clarence D.
2277 Fair Oaks Blvd., Suite 190
Sacramento, CA 95825
(916) 368-3955, voice

White, Pamela Britton, JD
850 Colorado Blvd., Suite 102
Los Angeles, CA 90041
(818) 796-1093, voice

Winslow, Suzanne Foster, LCSW
11261 Sutherland Lane
Capitola, CA 95010
(408) 476-0704, voice

Yardley, Stephen K.
2806 Bidwell St.
Davis, CA 95616
(916) 758-0431, voice

COLORADO

Agnew, Dixie N.
Mediation West
1000 Summit Blvd.
P.O. Box 60
Frisco, CO 80443
(303) 668-3001, voice
(303) 668-3108, fax

Bedell, Jean M.
CDR Associates
2142 Jordan Place
Boulder, CO 80304
(303) 443-4695, voice
(303) 443-0599, fax

Coates, Christine A., JD
4890 Riverbend Rd.
Boulder, CO 80301
(303) 443-8524, voice
(303) 786-8035, fax

Dragon, Larry D., MA
The Mediation Center
117 Aspen Airport Business
    Center, Suite 314
Aspen, CO 81611
(970) 920-7646, voice
(970) 925-5457, fax

Eaton, Janet R.
524 S. Cascade Ave., Suite 2
Colorado Springs, CO 80903
(719) 636-5123, voice
(719) 636-2077, fax

Golten, Mary Margaret
CDR Associates
100 Arapahoe Ave., #12
Boulder, CO 80302
(303) 442-7367, voice
(303) 442-7442, fax

Gutterman, Sheila, JD, MA
Law Office of Sheila Gutterman
400 S. Colorado Blvd., Suite 900
Denver, CO 80222
(303) 333-6670, voice
(303) 333-7769, fax

Harrison, Douglas S.
Ph7 Conflict Resolutions, Inc.
10600 W. Alameda, #U-6
Lakewood, CO 80226
(303) 986-3100, voice
(303) 986-3432, fax

Head, Katherine S., LCSW
The Center for Solutions
50 S. Steele St., Suite 800
Denver, CO 80209
(303) 329-3435, voice
(303) 299-5572, fax

Kerr, Linda Q., MS
331 Lodgewood Lane
Lafayette, CO 80026
(303) 604-6321, voice

Landa, Albert L.
Office of Dispute Resolution
1123 Custer Ave.
Colorado Springs, CO 80903
(719) 663-6680, voice
(719) 663-6680, fax

Maday, Michael J., MSW
Resolution Resources of
    Colorado
1335 Chambers Dr.
Colorado Spring, CO 80904
(719) 471-0970, voice

Mayer, Bernard
CDR Associates
100 Arapahoe Ave., #12
Boulder, CO 80302
(303) 442-7367, voice
(303) 442-7442, fax

McWilliams, Joan H., PC
Attorneys-at-Law
Dispute Resolution Services
1775 Sherman St., Suite 2825
Denver, CO 80203
(303) 830-0171, voice
(303) 830-8422, fax

Meltzer, Martin D., MA, LPC, NCC
6979 S. Holly Circle, Suite 190
Englewood, CO 80112
(303) 721-9779, voice
(303) 721-7350, fax

Meyrich, Steven
100 Arapahoe Ave., #14
Boulder, CO 80302
(303) 440-8238, voice
(303) 938-9703, fax

Nowak, Nancy Cohen, MA, LPC
2600 S. Parker Rd.
Building 7, Suite 270
Aurora, CO 80014
(303) 617-2677, voice
(303) 617-2672, fax

Rymers, John A., MA
1805 S. Bellaire St., Suite 301
Denver, CO 80219
(303) 759-5103, voice
(303) 757-4225, fax

Schultheis, Catherine M.
Paralegal Services & Mediation
P.O. Box 103
Niwot, CO 80544
(303) 652-3638, voice
(303) 652-3482, fax

Schwartz, William
Family Mediation Group
709 Clarkson St.
Denver, CO 80218
(303) 322-3080, voice
(303) 321-9473, fax

Smith, Thomas H., PhD
1336 Northridge Court
Boulder, CO 80304
(303) 444-0181, voice

Steinhardt, Roberta J., JD
Acceptable Terms Mediation
  Services
5353 W. Dartmouth Ave.,
  Suite 401
Denver, CO 80227
(303) 988-5191, voice

Swartz, Arnold L., LCSW
Arnold Swartz and Associates
720 Kipling St., #200
Lakewood, CO 80215
(303) 237-4828, voice
(303) 232-3892, fax

Taylor, Raymond
2004 N. 12th, #4
Grand Junction, CO 81501
(303) 242-6061, voice
(303) 243-8515, fax

Whicher, S. Wendy, MA, JD
Domestic Mediation
1911 Main Ave., Suite 222
Durango, CO 81301
(970) 259-7610, voice

CONNECTICUT

Aaron, Barbara D.
Whitehead & Aaron
241 Main St.
Hartford, CT 06106-8002
(203) 241-7797, voice
(203) 241-7744, fax

Becker, Michael R., JD
Mediation Offices of Michael
  Becker
2701 Summer St., Suite 200
Stamford, CT 06905
(203) 363-2248, voice
(203) 363-2249, fax

Carney, Mary Ann
Hutton-Carney Mediation Associates
55 Skyline Dr.
South Windsor, CT 06074
(860) 644-6308, voice
(860) 644-6308, fax

Fremed, Resa, MA, EdD
New England Counseling and
  Mediation
898 Ethan Allen Hwy.
Ridgefield, CT 06877
(203) 431-4957, voice
(203) 431-7984, fax

Friedman, Roberta S.
Mediation Center of Connecticut
383 Orange St.
New Haven, CT 06511
(203) 776-9002, voice
(203) 787-3259, fax

Marcus, Walter
Center for Divorce Mediation &
  Alternative Dispute Resolution,
  Inc.
P.O. Box 326
10 Wall St.
Norwalk, CT 06852
(203) 854-9394, voice
(203) 853-9246, fax

Robson, Bonnie C., JD
400 Washington St.
Gengras Building
Hartford, CT 06106
(203) 241-8035, voice
(203) 241-8045, fax

Robson, Kenneth S., MD
Institute of Living
400 Washington St.
Hartford, CT 06106
(203) 241-6891, voice
(203) 241-8045, fax

Schaefer, Bernice C., PhD
91 Duncaster Rd.
Bloomfield, CT 06002
(203) 243-9795, voice
(203) 242-7097, fax

Sienkiewicz, Nancy R.
Sienkiewicz & McKenna
9 S. Main St.
P.O. Box 786
New Milford, CT 06776
(203) 354-1583, voice
(203) 355-4439, fax

Strong, Leslie, PhD
46 Overlook Rd.
Glastonbury, CT 06033
(203) 633-6176, voice
(203) 657-3531, fax

Von Schmidt, Georgia, JD
37 Arch St.
Greenwich, CT 06830
(203) 622-5900, voice
(203) 622-8298, fax

Wasserman, Elga R., JD
192 Bishop St.
New Haven, CT 06511
(203) 773-9000, voice
(203) 787-3259, fax

White, Flora
State of Connecticut, Superior
    Court
Family Relations Division
235 Church St.
New Haven, CT 06510
(203) 789-7903, voice

Widing, Carol
Carol Widing, Attorney at Law
Mediated Divorce Services
185 Asylum St., Suite 3100
Hartford, CT 06103
(203) 678-8401, voice
(203) 678-8223, fax

DELAWARE

Clarkson-Shorter, Jolly
Tressler Mediation Services
1007 White Birch Dr.
Newark, DE 19713
(302) 738-9702, voice

FLORIDA

Bravo, Carmine
2957 W. Hwy. 434, Suite 400
Longwood, FL 32779
(407) 774-1686, voice
(407) 774-7130, fax

Crowell, Merrie-Roxie, MA, JD
1367 Fairfield Dr.
Clearwater, FL 34624
(813) 535-8555, voice

Davis, Joseph W.
Davis, Monk & Company
4010 NW 25th Place
Gainsville, FL 32606
(904) 372-6300, voice
(904) 375-1583, fax

DiGennaro, Iris B., Esq.
9131 College Parkway
Suite 13B, Box 225
Fort Myers, FL 33919
(813) 481-9683, voice

Doelker, Richard E., Jr.
4555 Lavallet Lane
Pensacola, FL 32504
(904) 474-2688, voice
(904) 474-3131, fax

Dorian, Phyllis
3147 Hyde Park Dr.
Clearwater, FL 34621
(813) 787-9627, voice

Finman, Sheldon E., JD
Divorce Mediation Services
2215 First St.
Ft. Myers, FL 33901
(813) 332-4543, voice
(813) 334-7828, fax

Firestone, Gregory
USF Mediation Institute
2901 W. Busch Blvd., Suite 707
Tampa, FL 33618
(813) 933-7655, voice
(813) 975-4816, fax

Gianino, Peter T.
The Law Offices of Grazi,
   Gianino, and Cohen
217 East Ocean Blvd.
Stuart, FL 34994
(407) 286-0200, voice
(407) 286-4789, fax .

Gillette, Donald R., JD, PhD
Family Mediation Center
1006 N. Armenia
Tampa, FL 33607
(813) 877-1210, voice
(813) 876-5966, fax

Godard, Diane R., PhD
3450 E. Lake Rd., Suite 305
Palm Harbor, FL 34685
(813) 785-1820, voice
(813) 781-5735, fax

Kaslow, Florence W., PhD
Kaslow Associates, PA
2161 Palm Beach Lakes Blvd.
Raymond Office Plaza, Suite 216
West Palm Beach, FL 33409
(407) 625-0288, voice
(407) 832-3153, fax

Koedam, Wilhelmina S., PhD
1021 Ives Dairy Rd.
Building 3, Suite 212
North Miami Beach, FL 33179
(305) 653-0098, voice
(305) 654-4412, fax

Lake, Larry B., PhD
Counseling and Mediation
  Center
P.O. Box 1379
St. Augustine, FL 32085
(904) 824-2501, voice

Percher, Martin L., LCSW
3787 Caramabola Circle North
Coconut Beach, FL 33066
(407) 852-3333, voice

Rubin, Melvin A.
Law Offices of Melvin, Alvin &
  Rubin
111 Majorca Ave., #A
Coral Gables, FL 33134
(305) 446-4630, voice
(305) 446-4978, fax

Scholz-Rubin, Susan, PhD
Divorce & Family Mediation
  Center
111 Majorca Ave., #B
Coral Gables, FL 33134
(305) 445-7445, voice
(305) 448-0687, fax

Schreiber, Lee A., Esq.
Thompson & Schreiber, PA
3949 Evans Ave., Suite 206
Fort Myers, FL 33901
(813) 936-5225, voice
(813) 936-2542, fax

Sherr, Linda B., MA
504 Payne Parkway
Sarasota, FL 34237
(813) 955-1330, voice
(813) 955-4163, fax

Warner, Daniel K.
Mediation Resource Center
4741 Atlantic Blvd., #C
Jacksonville, FL 32207
(904) 399-4113, voice

Waxman, Geraldine Lee, JD
9780 N.W. 16th St.
Plantation, FL 33322
(305) 472-7458, voice
(305) 476-5677, fax

Weinberger, Hedy Lehrer
Hillsborough County Family
  Diversion
Main Court House
419 Pierce St., Rm. 230
Tampa, FL 33602
(813) 272-5642, voice
(813) 272-5887, fax

GEORGIA

Berlin, Robert A.
Decision Management Associates
3081 Revere Court
Atlanta, GA 30340
(404) 458-7808, voice
(404) 455-7272, fax

Close, Nancy Thompson, MEd
104 Ansley Villa Dr., N.E.
Atlanta, GA 30324
(404) 892-4827, voice

Foster, Nancy
Center for Counseling &
  Psychological Services
2321 Henry Clower Blvd., Suite A
Snellville, GA 30278
(404) 979-0892, voice
(404) 978-2255, fax

Giese, Kay A.
Sweat & Giese, PA
P.O. Box 1626
Athens, GA 30603
(706) 549-0500, voice
(706) 543-8453, fax

Herrman, Margaret S., PhD
Carl Vinson Institute of
  Government
The University of Georgia
201 N. Milledge Ave.
Athens, GA 30602
(706) 542-2736, voice

Keim, Timothy A.
7848 Princess Dr.
Jonesboro, GA 30236
(770) 603-0506, voice
(770) 473-0075, fax

Kitchens, Marti P., MA
7193 Douglas Blvd., #103
Douglasville, GA 30135
(404) 942-9361, voice
(404) 947-9840, fax

Ma'luf, Jan
P.O. Box 3403
LaGrange, GA 30241-3403
(706) 883-2168, voice
(706) 883-2169, fax

Manley, E. Elizabeth, MEd, JD
Atlanta Divorce Mediators
1149 Austin Ave. N.E.
Atlanta, GA 30307
(404) 378-3238, voice
(404) 577-6505, fax

Marth, Kathryn
Atlanta Divorce Mediators
150 E. Ponce De Leon, Suite 460
Decatur, GA 30030
(404) 378-3238, voice

Pierce, Lemoine D., MEd, JD
School for Dispute Resolution
P.O. Box 2372
Decatur, GA 30031-2372
(404) 299-1128, voice
(404) 261-2017, fax

Schaffer, Beverly K., PhD
1105-C Clairmont Ave.
Decatur, GA 30030-1256
(404) 634-6394, voice
(404) 727-4639, fax

Simon, Ted F.
Divorce Mediation of Cobb
  County
670 Village Trace Bldg.,
  #100
Marietta, GA 30067
(404) 980-0988, voice
(404) 977-8899, fax

Stoker, Norman M.
Peaceful Resolutions, Inc.
P.O. Box 813126
Smyrna, GA 30081-3126
(770) 432-0212, voice

HAWAII

Shapiro, Gerald F.
West Hawaii Mediation Services
21 Puako Beach Dr.
Kamuela, HI 96743
(808) 882-1565, voice
(808) 882-1565, fax

Shapiro, Joan
West Hawaii Mediation Services
21 Puako Beach Dr.
Kamuela, HI 96743
(808) 882-1565, voice
(808) 882-1565, fax

IDAHO

Brown, Patricia Crete, MSW
Director
Heartland Centers Inc.
303 North 12th Ave.
Pocatello, ID 83201
(208) 234-1099, voice
(208) 234-1100, fax

Hawley, Victoria, MSW
3221 N. 28th St.
Boise, ID 83703
(208) 336-9366, voice
(208) 336-1451, fax

Knudson, Barbara, PhD
623 W. Hays
Boise, ID 83702
(208) 336-1472, voice

Meyer, Marie, EdD
1454 Shenandoah Dr.
Boise, ID 83712
(208) 336-7278, voice
(208) 336-7278, fax

Thompson, Frances H., JD
North Idaho Family Mediation
　Services
116 E. Third St., Suite 201
P.O. Box 8489
Moscow, ID 83843
(208) 882-6856, voice
(208) 882-6856, fax

Werth, Wendy Werner
Werth & Werth Mediation
P.O. Box 985
Sun Valley, ID 83353
(208) 788-9781, voice

ILLINOIS

Beck, Peggy Glazier, LCSW
3330 Old Glenview Rd., Suite 15
Wilmette, IL 60091
(847) 256-2300, voice

Becker-Warden, Sandra, LCSW,
　ACSW
Family Life Consultants
3C Meadow Heights Professional
　Park
Collinsville, IL 62234
(618) 345-9536, voice

Biank, Nancee M., MSW, ACSW,
　LCSW
Partners in Transition
832 The Pines
Hinsdale, IL 60521
(708) 256-2300, voice
(708) 636-3410, fax

Borland, Kathleen Landreth
Marriage Family Counseling
505 N. Lake Shore Dr., #2708
Chicago, IL 60611
(312) 345-8822, voice
(312) 345-8801, fax

Bruer, David Cavan
PACTS
P.O. Box 1043
151 N. 4th St., #1
DeKalb, IL 60115
(815) 748-3237, voice
(815) 748-5437, fax

Collins, Elaine L.
1590 S. Milwaukee Ave.,
　Suite 228
Libertyville, IL 60048
(847) 680-9848, voice
(847) 680-3607, fax

Daskal, Frona C., JD
The Mediation Group
155 N. Michigan Ave., #700
Chicago, IL 60601
(312) 565-6565, voice

Gay, Pat, MS
P.O. Box 4322
Fairview Heights, IL 62208
(618) 277-1844, voice

Gentry, Deborah Barnes
Illinois State University
Dept. of Family and Consumer
  Science
203 J. Turner Hall
Normal, IL 61790-5060
(309) 438-7935, voice
(309) 438-5037, fax

Good, Diana D., MA
2123 O'Donnell Dr.
Champaign, IL 61821
(217) 359-7052, voice

Hammer, Don C.
202 N. Center St.
Bloomington, IL 61701
(309) 828-7331, voice
(309) 827-7423, fax

Harnish, Robert Brunk, DMin
736 Dobson St., #3E
Evanston, IL 60202
(708) 475-1642, voice

Hogan, Judy L.
Attorney at Law
115 Campbell Street, Suite 100
Geneva, IL 60134
(708) 208-9982, voice
(708) 232-1890, fax

Jacob, Lynn Carp, LCSW
Family & Legal Social Services
2234 Asbury Ave.
Evanston, IL 60201
(847) 866-6231, voice
(847) 866-6718, fax

Jann, Earl B., PhD
Affiliates in Mediation
633 Skokie Blvd., Suite 400A
Northbrook, IL 60062
(708) 564-9900, voice
(708) 480-0088, fax

Kelly, Margaret
The Counselors' Office
3841 W. 95th St.
Evergreen Park, IL 60642
(708) 535-2777, voice

Kennedy, Susan, MA, LCSW
2420 Isabella
Evanston, IL 60201
(708) 475-1059, voice
(312) 527-0450, fax

Kessler, Jerald A., JD
1950 Sheridan Rd., Suite 101
Highland Park, IL 60035
(847) 433-2323, voice
(847) 433-2349, fax

London, William A., JD
4250 N. Marine Dr., #402
Chicago, IL 60613-1721
(312) 472-7673, voice
(312) 975-0145, fax

Massaquoi, Joan Elizabeth
360 E. Randolph
Chicago, IL 60601
(312) 240-1267, voice
(312) 240-1385, fax

Mindrup, Bruce P., MA
Mediation Services of Mid-Illinois
106 Goodrich St.
Jerseyville, IL 62052
(618) 498-4911, voice
(618) 498-4921, fax

Mitchell, Roberta King
18552 Argyle Ave.
Homewood, IL 60430
(708) 799-7193, voice

Nelson, Mary E.
Chicago Mediation Group
2733 W. Ainslie
Chicago, IL 60625
(312) 907-9470, voice
(312) 907-9470, fax

Powers, Margaret S.
415 W. Gold Rd., Suite 22
Arlington Heights, IL 60005
(312) 943-2155, x6, voice
(708) 670-0036, fax

Sudduth, Debra
1906 Oakwood Ave.
Bloomington, IL 61704
(309) 664-0556, voice
(309) 662-8821, fax

Zoub, Burton I., JD
155 N. Michigan Ave., #600
Chicago, IL 60601
(312) 938-0011, voice
(312) 938-8541, fax

INDIANA

Long, Linda L.
Strategies Inc.
460 Bote Dr.
Porter, IN 46304
(219) 464-2940, voice
(219) 926-4485, fax

Maass, Vera S., PhD
Living Skills Institute
8204 Westfield Blvd.
Indianapolis, IN 46240
(317) 232-6501, voice

Mitchell-Dix, Janet E.
Mediator
Oak Valley N. Professional Bldg.
5517 Oak Valley Place, Suite 205
Fort Wayne, IN 46845
(219) 483-7660, voice
(219) 483-7660, fax

Newton, Ann Kelly, MSW, ACSW
501 N. Arlington St.
Greencastle, IN 46135
(317) 653-3856, voice
(317) 653-3856, fax

Purvis, Margaret
Behavioral Health Care
  Associates
P.O. Box 104
600 Promenade
Richmond, IN 47374
(317) 983-8079, voice
(317) 966-8690, fax

Smith, Riette Thomas, MS
Therapy/Mediation
P.O. Box 1965
Bloomington, IN 47402-1965
(812) 332-2558, voice
(812) 332-2557, fax

Tuttle, Deborah M.
Attorney
300 N. Michigan Ave., Suite 219
South Bend, IN 46601
(219) 288-5100, voice
(219) 282-4344, fax

IOWA

Tarrance, Crevon, MSW
2239 Taylor Dr.
Iowa City, IA 52240
(319) 338-0388, voice

KANSAS

Fairchild, Robert W.
Riling, Burkhead, Fairchild &
  Nitcher
P.O. Box B
Lawrence, KS 66044
(913) 841-4700, voice
(913) 843-0161, fax

Hughes, Nancy, PhD, LCSW
University of Kansas
Psychological Clinic
Lawrence, KS 66045
(913) 864-4121, voice
(913) 864-5224, fax

Kretchmer, Gary
Domestic Court Services
905 W. Spruce
Olathe, KS 66061
(913) 782-7252, voice
(913) 782-3297, fax

Morphis, Doug
Counseling and Mediation
  Center
334 N. Topeka
Wichita, KS 67202
(316) 269-2322, voice
(316) 269-2448, fax

KENTUCKY

Colley, Rose T.
410 W. Chestnut, Suite 356
Louisville, KY 40202-2323
(502) 581-1961, voice
(502) 581-9832, fax

Lichtenstein, Israel, EdD
Lichtenstein Consulting
46 Gunpowder Ridge
Fort Thomas, KY 41075
(606) 781-0717, voice

Llewellyn, John J., JD
Family Mediation Service of
  Kentucky
3711 Hillsdale Rd.
Louisville, KY 40222
(502) 426-8161, voice
(502) 581-1644, fax

McCann, John D.
Attorney at Law
Chevy Chase Plaza
836 East Euclid Ave., Suite 317
Lexington, KY 40502
(606) 269-4525, voice
(606) 268-9141, fax

Parsons-Rulli, Peggy
2 Dortha Ave.
Florence, KY 41042
(606) 525-1487, voice
(606) 525-7170, fax

Weiss, Terry
Council on Peacemaking
1306 Willow Ave.
Louisville, KY 40204
(502) 456-6454, voice
(502) 485-0782, fax

Zerhusen, Karen A., PSC
Attorney–Mediator
178 Barnwood Dr., Suite 107
Edgewood, KY 41017
(606) 331-2558, voice
(606) 344-1466, fax

LOUISIANA

Lipscomb, Nell I., MSW, JD
The Mediation Center
3117 7th St., Second Floor
Metaine, LA 70002
(504) 861-0505, voice
(504) 838-7030, fax

Morris, Edith H.
1515 Poydras St., Suite 1870
New Orleans, LA 70112
(504) 524-3781, voice
(504) 561-0228, fax

Prosser Davis, Laura
The Mediation Center
7737 Old Hammond Hwy., Suite
  B-4
Baton Rouge, LA 70809
(504) 926-0776, voice
(504) 926-0021, fax

MAINE

Anthony, Cushman D.
120 Exchange St., Suite 208
Portland, ME 04101
(207) 775-3091, voice
(207) 775-7078, fax

Chase, Lloyd R.
President
Houlton Consulting Group
106 Main St.
P.O. Box 323
Houlton, ME 04730-0323
(207) 532-2176, voice
(207) 532-4039, fax

Clark, Jacqui
Mediation and Facilitation
  Resources
71 Winthrop St.
Augusta, ME 04330
(207) 622-1429, voice

MARYLAND

Bermant, Lili
The Concordia Systems Group
11029 Seven Hill Lane
Potomac, MD 20854
(301) 983-8707, voice
(301) 983-8707, fax

Butler, Aza Howard
The Custody & Mediation
  Division
801 Dairy Rd.
P.O. Box 538
Parkton, MD 21120
(410) 887-6570, voice
(410) 887-4806, fax

Crockett, Catherine Grayson
Attorney/Mediator
966 Hungerford Dr.,
  Suite 31-B
Rockville, MD 20850
(301) 279-6720, voice
(301) 279-6904, fax

Garron, Rachel S.
Potomac Mediation Group
4919 Hampden Lane
Bethesda, MD 20814
(301) 652-6654, voice

Girdner, Linda K., PhD
2324 Maytime Dr.
Gambrills, MD 21054
(202) 662-1722, voice
(202) 662-1755, fax

Goldberg, David S.
Family Mediation Services, Inc.
255 N. Washington St., #200
Rockville, MD 20850
(301) 279-7500, voice
(301) 279-7521, fax

Grebe, Sarah Childs, MEd, MA
Family Center for Mediation &
  Counseling
3514 Players Mill Rd., Suite 100
Kensington, MD 20895
(301) 946-3400, voice
(301) 946-3400, fax

Hackett, Sylvia L., JD
Attorney at Law
1701 Edmondson Ave., #202
Catonsville, MD 21228-4346
(410) 747-6840, voice
(410) 788-1278, fax

Halvorsen, Diane L.
8018 Quarry Ridge Way
Bethesda, MD 20817
(301) 469-9637, voice

Ketcham, Robert C., JD
Lifebridge Family Mediation
7104 Exfair Rd.
Bethesda, MD 20814
(301) 215-7933, voice

Kobren, Martin
Mediation Resources, LLC
7475 Wisconsin Ave., #500
Bethesda, MD 20814
(301) 718-2422, voice

Kranitz, Martin Alan, MA
Mediation Services of Annapolis
1160 Spa Rd., 1-B
Annapolis, MD 21403
(800) 781-7500, voice
(410) 974-8888, fax

Murphy, Peter F.
P.O. Box 119
Bryans Rd., MD 20616
(301) 283-0947, voice
(301) 375-8433, fax

Quinlan, Robert E.
Attorney at Law
8 Virginia Dr.
Gaithersburg, MD 20877
(301) 840-2022, voice
(301) 963-4105, fax

Rodbell, Stanley L., JD, LCSW
10541 Catterskill Court
Columbia, MD 21044
(410) 730-2211, voice
(410) 730-7618, fax

Schneider, Carl D., PhD
Mediation Matters
3917 Dunnel Lane
Kensington, MD 20895
(301) 933-8880, voice
(301) 933-9097, fax

Seymour, Shirley Pittman, JD
11907 Henry Fleet Dr.
Potomac, MD 20854
(301) 340-1477, voice
(301) 340-2942, fax

Simon, Phyllis B., MPA
Family & Child Associates
414 Hungerford Dr., #240
Rockville, MD 20850
(301) 340-2060, voice
(301) 984-3325, fax

Smith, David J., JD
19 Kirwin Court
Parkville, MD 21234
(410) 836-4434, voice
(410) 836-4198, fax

Stovall, Lois H.
Crockett & Stovall
P.O. Box 2123
Silver Spring, MD 20901
(301) 495-2991, voice

Sulami, Susan, JD
Lifebridge Family Mediation
7104 Exfair Rd.
Bethesda, MD 20814
(301) 215-7933, voice

Tong, Elizabeth B.
108 N. Washington St.
Easton, MD 21601
(410) 822-5993, voice
(410) 822-5993, fax

Vernon, Maureen
Bay Region Counseling Services
3006 Solomons Island Rd.
Edgewater, MD 21037
(410) 266-0019, voice
(410) 266-0019, fax

Weiner, Bertram I., JD, MPA
Bertel Counseling and Mediation
   Service
11408 Fairoak Dr.
Silver Spring, MD 20902
(301) 593-7744, voice
(301) 593-3921, fax

Williams, Elizabeth Z., JD
Mediation Resources
7475 Wisconsin Ave., Suite 500
Bethesda, MD 20814
(301) 657-1011, voice

Yee, Anna, MSW
9219 Oregold Court
Laurel, MD 20708
(301) 725-3954, voice
(301) 497-1966, fax

MASSACHUSETTS

Berkowitz, June F.
73 Atlantic Rd.
Gloucester, MA 01930-3241
(508) 281-3910, voice

Bowling, G. Daniel, JD
246 Long Pond Rd.
Great Barrington, MA 01230
(413) 528-5377, voice

Clarkin, Bruce D.
Dispute Mediation, Inc.
95 State St.
Springfield, MA 01103
(413) 788-8981, voice

Fischer, S. Tracy, Esq.
99 Washington St.
Salem, MA 01970
(505) 745-0590, voice
(508) 744-5151, fax

Fish, Deborah Ann
48 Doane Rd.
Chatham, MA 02633
(508) 945-3073, voice
(508) 945-5022, fax

Fiske, John
Healy, Fiske and Woodbury
189 Cambridge St.
Cambridge, MA 02141-1279
(617) 354-7133, voice
(617) 354-5830, fax

Gross, Steven
97 Franklin St.
Greenfield, MA 01301
(413) 772-6080, voice

Kunstman, Earl, MA
68 S. Main St.
Natick, MA 01760
(508) 651-2756, voice
(508) 653-2271, fax

Neumann, Diane, JD, MA
Divorce Mediation Services
650 Worcester Rd.
Framingham, MA 01701-5248
(508) 879-9095, voice
(508) 879-9099, fax

Perlman, Gail L., MSW, JD
Dispute Mediation, Inc.
237 Main St., Suite 4
Northampton, MA 01060-3139
(413) 585-0977, voice
(413) 585-0999, fax

Weinberger, Janet B.
206 Windsor Rd.
Newton, MA 02168
(617) 965-4432, voice
(617) 527-3536, fax

Woolner, Catherine
Franklin Mediation Service
97 Franklin St.
Greenfield, MA 01301
(413) 774-7469, voice
(413) 773-3834, fax

Younger, Barbara C., Esq.
152R Main St.
Wenham, MA 01984
(508) 468-2226, voice
(508) 468-3801, fax

MICHIGAN

Bishop, Elizabeth S., PhD
Arbor Psychological Consultants
1565 Eastover Place
Ann Arbor, MI 48104
(313) 741-8844, voice
(313) 741-9038, fax

Blume, Thomas W., PhD
Montgomery & Associates
1400 Woodward Ave., Suite 40
Bloomfield Hills, MI 48304
(810) 642-8042, voice

Clark, Beverly
Mediation Works
440 E. Congress, Suite 4R
Detroit, MI 48226-2917
(313) 961-4440, voice
(313) 961-5830, fax

Marsh, Gary L.
Ann Arbor Mediation Center
330 E. Liberty, #3A
Ann Arbor, MI 48104
(313) 663-1155, voice
(313) 663-0524, fax

Mikusko, M. Brady
Ann Arbor Mediation Center
330 E. Liberty, #3A
Ann Arbor, MI 48104
(313) 663-1155, voice

Nichols, Margaret J., JD
Nichols, Sacks, Slank & Sweet
121 W. Washington St., #300
Ann Arbor, MI 48104
(313) 994-3000, voice
(313) 994-1557, fax

Whiteside, Mary F., PhD
Ann Arbor Center for the Family
2300 Washtenaw Ave., Suite 203
Ann Arbor, MI 48104
(313) 995-5181, voice
(313) 995-9011, fax

Williams, Carl E., EdD
1860 Robert St.
Ann Arbor, MI 48104
(317) 846-4937, voice

Zumeta, Zena D., JD
Ann Arbor Mediation Center
330 E. Liberty, #3A
Ann Arbor, MI 48104
(313) 663-1155, voice
(313) 663-0524, fax

MINNESOTA

Ackerman, Mary
1725 Wellesley Ave.
St. Paul, MN 55105
(612) 690-3841, voice
(612) 698-7222, fax

Erickson, Stephen K., JD
Erickson Mediation Institute
850 Northland Plaza
3800 W. 80th St.
Minneapolis, MN 55431
(612) 835-3688, voice
(612) 835-3689, fax

Frederickson, Jeanette
3700 Piper Jaffray Tower
Minneapolis, MN 55402
(612) 339-7300, voice
(612) 336-2940, fax

Goodwyne, Lucille M., MSN
5525 Timber Lane
Excelsior, MN 55331
(612) 470-0093, voice

Hanson, Freya Ottem
625 Silver Lake Rd.
St. Paul, MN 55112
(612) 633-9408, voice
(612) 633-1173, fax

Hausken, Terje
RR 2, Box 17X
Pine Island, MN 55963
(507) 281-9295, voice

Leick, Christine M.
Dispute Resolution Services
2500 One Financial Plaza
120 S. 6th St.

Minneapolis, MN 55402
(612) 349-5252, voice
(612) 349-9242, fax

Mainzer, Susan D.
Conflict Management Providers
3033 Humboldt Ave. S.
Minneapolis, MN 55408
(612) 824-7664, voice
(612) 824-7664, fax

McKnight, Marilyn, MA
Executive Director
Erickson Mediation Institute
850 Northland Plaza
3800 W. 80th St.
Minneapolis, MN 55431
(612) 835-1564, voice
(612) 835-3689, fax

Nyquist, Dean A.
Family Conflict Resolution
  Center
5637 Brooklyn Blvd., #200
Brooklyn Center, MN 55429
(612) 533-7272, voice
(612) 533-3183, fax

Tisserand, Marilyn J., LP
Lakes Area Counseling &
  Mediation
110 6th Ave. E.
P.O. Box 1254
Alexandria, MN 56308
(612) 763-9000, voice

Westfall, Victoria
9833 Colorado Circle
Bloomington, MN 55438
(612) 835-0554, voice

MISSOURI

Amato, Susan L., JD
130 S. Bemiston, #706
Clayton, MO 63105
(314) 862-0330, voice
(314) 727-5464, fax

Benjamin, Robert D., MSW, JD
Mediation & Conflict
  Management Services
8000 Bonhomme, Suite 201
St. Louis, MO 63105
(314) 721-4333, voice
(314) 721-6845, fax

Brockett, Michael L.
Southwest Mediation Clinics, Inc.
3937 College View Dr.
Joplin, MO 64801
(417) 782-1846, voice
(417) 782-4556, fax

Devine, Donna L.
Director
Domestic Relations Programs
Jackson County Missouri Family
  Court
2729 Gillham Rd.
Kansas City, MO 64108-3112
(816) 881-6526, voice
(816) 881-6504, fax

Frager, Julius Z., JD, MBA
Alternative Solutions, Inc.
13112 Piedmont Court
St. Louis, MO 63043
(314) 434-4200, voice
(314) 434-2768, fax

Freed, Alan E., JD
Paule Camazine & Blumenthal
  P.C.
165 N. Meramec, 6th Floor
Clayton, MO 63105
(314) 727-2266, voice
(314) 727-2101, fax

Kiser, Mary Anne, MA
Kiser Counseling Services
411 Nichols Rd., Suite 217
Kansas City, MO 64112
(816) 931-9912, voice
(816) 561-5352, fax

Love, Kakie
Families in Transition
5413 Dalcross Dr.
Columbia, MO 65203
(573) 443-7717, voice
(573) 449-9505, fax

Malley, Lynn M., JD
200 N. Ninth St., Suite A
Columbia, MO 65201
(314) 499-0748, voice
(314) 499-4469, fax

Mulhearn, Michael, PhD
2100 N. Noland Rd.
Independence, MO 64050
(816) 254-9000, voice
(816) 836-9922, fax

Stewart, Betsy Ann T.
Ahmann, Stewart & Nixon
1520Q E. 23rd St.
P.O. Box 357
Independence, MO 64051
(816) 461-5858, voice
(816) 461-2465, fax

Ver Dught, ElGene, JD
Mediation Services of Missouri
3600 S. Noland Rd., Suite A
Independence, MO 64055
800-637-7511
(816) 836-4141, voice
(816) 461-6022, fax

MONTANA

Andes, Roy H.
Wilmot & Andes
305 E. Alder St.
Missoula, MT 59802
(406) 728-7295, voice

Lusse, Arthur W.
201 W. Main, Suite 104
Missoula, MT 59802
(406) 543-1113, voice
(406) 543-1157, fax

Lusse, Katherine
Montana Mediators
201 W. Main, Suite 104
Missoula, MT 59802
(406) 543-1113, voice
(406) 543-1157, fax

NORTH DAKOTA

Olsen, Glenn W., PhD
The Mediation Center
421 Demers Ave.
Grand Forks, ND 58202
(701) 777-3145, voice
(701) 772-0233, fax

NEBRASKA

Lamberty, Patricia A.
Lamberty P.C.
320 N. 68th St.
Omaha, NE 68132
(402) 556-5808, voice
(402) 558-1929, fax

NEVADA

Bengtson, Patti
2359 Wide Horizon Dr.
Reno, NV 89509
(702) 328-3830, voice

Bushard, Phil
Family Mediation Program
75 Court St.
Reno, NV 89501
(702) 328-3556, voice
(702) 328-3548, fax

Coyne, Patricia Hellmund, MA,
   LSW
Ecker and Standish Chartered
Bank of America Plaza
300 S. 4th St., #611
Las Vegas, NV 89101
(702) 384-1700, voice
(702) 384-8150, fax

Kiffer, Charlotte S., MS
Alternative Solutions
333 N. Rancho Dr., #138
Las Vegas, NV 89106
(702) 646-2645, voice

Meyer, Joy D., MS
Mediator Substance Abuse
   Counselor
6200 S. Virginia St.
Reno, NV 89511
(702) 851-0913, voice
(702) 828-6200, fax

Rivard, Charlene
5317 Westleigh
Las Vegas, NV 89102
(702) 878-5396, voice

Urban, Ruth Pearson, MS
Clark County Neighborhood
   Justice Center
1600 Pinto Lane
Las Vegas, NV 89106
(702) 455-5722, voice
(702) 455-5950, fax

NEW HAMPSHIRE

Dochstader, Candace
Nashua Mediation Program
18 Mulberry St.
Nashua, NH 03060
(603) 594-3330, voice
(603) 594-3452, fax

Elise, Francoise, MSW
Divorce & Family Mediation
   Services
114 Bay St.
Manchester, NH 03104
(603) 627-0525, voice
(603) 627-0525, fax

Hill, Rose M.
New Hampshire Mediation
  Program, Inc.
280 Pleasant St., H-3
Concord, NH 03301-2553
(603) 224-8043, voice
(603) 224-8388, fax

Ruel, Olivia A., PhD
Alternative Center for Mediation
  & Training
4 Felt Rd.
Keene, NH 03431
(800) 891-7931, voice
(603) 358-1081, fax

NEW JERSEY

Bean, Ralph
145 Wellington Ave.
Pleasantville, NJ 08232
(609) 484-9736, voice
(609) 718-5515, fax

Farley, Robert J.
Mediation Associates
31 Greenbrook Dr.
West Milford, NJ 07480
(201) 728-5427, voice

Fish, Linda, Esq.
New Jersey Mediation Associates
157 Engle St.
Englewood, NJ 07631
(201) 567-0003, voice
(201) 567-7809, fax

Forlenza, Samuel G., MA, PhD
207 Manor Ave.
Harrison, NJ 07029-2017
(201) 621-5060, voice

Friedland, Ruth W., Esq.
1107 Goffle Rd.
Hawthorne, NJ 07507
(201) 423-4200, voice
(201) 423-6074, fax

Hillman, Gail, Esq.
100 Northfield Ave.
West Orange, NJ 07052
(201) 669-2811, voice
(201) 669-2838, fax

Holman, Adele M., DSW
95 Dana Place
Englewood, NJ 07631-3629
(201) 567-2202, voice

Kressel, Kenneth
324 Raritan Ave.
Highland Park, NJ 08904
(908) 572-5444, voice

Margulies, Sam
45 Park St.
Montclair, NJ 07042
(201) 783-5515, voice
(201) 655-0016, fax

Muise, Madeline, MSW, LCSW
104-110 Maple Ave.
Red Bank, NJ 07701
(908) 530-2951, voice
(908) 576-8197, fax

Simpson, Gerald, JD
229 Washington St.
Toms River, NJ 08753
(908) 244-5300, voice
(908) 244-6745, fax

Wells, Mary Vivian Fu, MSW
Wells Consultation Service
36 June Place
Matawan, NJ 07747
(908) 583-1620, voice
(908) 583-5532, fax

NEW MEXICO

Anthony, Kathleen Burke
P.O. Box 26721
Albuquerque, NM 87125-6721
(505) 256-2552, voice

Beyer, Roberta
1228 Central S.W.
Albuquerque, NM 87102
(505) 243-1761, voice
(505) 243-3567, fax

Ginsberg, Terry A.
Second Judicial District
Family Court Clinic
P.O. Box 488
Albuquerque, NM 87103
(505) 841-7409, voice

Hopkins, Paul E., DMin
Samaritan Counseling Center
217 Locust N.E.
Albuquerque, NM 87102
(505) 842-5300, voice

Johnston, Retta
Rt. 4, Box 15C
Santa Fe, NM 87501
(505) 982-2983, voice

Sidwell, Jean Ann
New Mexico Center for Dispute
    Resolution
1520B Paseo de Peralta
Santa Fe, NM 87501
(505) 988-4578, voice

Stern, Paula, MA
Second Judicial District Court
    Clinic
P.O. Box 488
Albuquerque, NM 87103
(505) 841-7409, voice

Welsh, Mary McAnaw, EdD
P.O. Box 3483
Las Cruces, NM 88003
(505) 522-3066, voice

NEW YORK

Abel, Steven L.
2 New Hempstead Rd.
New City, NY 10956
(914) 633-4283, voice
(914) 634-1675, fax

Angelini, Constance J., JD
3809 Snowden Hill Rd.
New Hartford, NY 13413
(315) 737-9287, voice

Barsky, Morna, CSW
877 Lorenz Ave.
Baldwin, NY 11510
(516) 223-2025, voice

Blaise, Anne M.
Mediation Center of Rochester
2024 W. Henrietta Rd., Suite 5-G
Rochester, NY 14623
(716) 272-1990, voice
(716) 272-1978, fax

Brown, Susan J.
Family & Divorce Mediation
    Service
319 N. Tioga St.
Ithaca, NY 14850
(607) 272-8837, voice

Brumley, Charlene K., BSW
Buffalo Mediation Associates
4367 Harlem Rd.
Amherst, NY 14226
(716) 839-0040, voice
(716) 839-1983, fax

Collins, Robert Kirkman, Esq.
551 Fifth Ave., Suite 1704
New York, NY 10176
(212) 692-9222, voice
(212) 692-9229, fax

Connelly, Patricia A., MA, JD
Mediation Center
Clifton Executive Park
1741 Rt. 9
Clifton Park, NY 12065
(518) 371-6830, voice

Eckhaus, Naomi S., MS
Gateway Mediation Service
56 Hutchinson Blvd.
Scarsdale, NY 10583
(914) 725-1244, voice

Feer, Michael
New Justice
1153 W. Fayette, Suite 301
Syracuse, NY 13204
(315) 472-3171, voice
(315) 472-9252, fax

Fleisher, Marc
Brooklyn Law School
878 West End Ave.
New York, NY 10025-4956
(718) 780-7983, voice
(718) 780-0376, fax

Fohs, Mark William
1294 Richard Rd.
Skaneateles, NY 13152-8915
(315) 673-1001, voice

Friedman, Doris Toltz, JD
11 Martine Ave.
White Plains, NY 10606
(914) 997-6363, voice
(914) 997-2143, fax

Gardner, Nancy
10 Riverview Place
Hastings-on-Hudson, NY 10706
(914) 478-2973, voice
(914) 478-1493, fax

Gittelman, Diana B., Esq.
69 E. 89th St.
New York, NY 10128
(212) 426-2288, voice
(212) 426-2277, fax

Goodwin, Walter W.
12 Princess Lane
Londonville, NY 12211
(518) 434-1891, voice

Gordon, Lisa, JD
Albany Family & Divorce
  Mediation Center
16 Groesbeck Place
Delmar, NY 12054
(518) 439-6900, voice
(518) 439-8233, fax

Gulino, Lawrence C., MA,
  ACMFC
Divorce Mediation Center of
  Suffolk County
Four Freshman Lane
Stony Brook, NY 11790
(516) 751-3813, voice

Hamma, Judith M., MA
54 Brookline Ave.
Elmira, NY 14905
(607) 733-2765, voice

Handin, Kenneth H.
18 Seeley Dr.
Albany, NY 12203
(518) 573-3561, voice

Haynes, John M., PhD
146 Bayview Ave.
Northport, NY 11768-1509
(516) 757-4548, voice
(516) 757-4548, fax

Heilmann, Ronald W., ACSW,
  CSW
Mediation Network of Syracuse
1940 Valley Dr.
Syracuse, NY 13207
(315) 492-1082, voice

Heister, John W., PhD
Mediation Center of Rochester
2024 W. Henrietta Rd., Suite 5-G
Rochester, NY 14623
(716) 272-1990, voice
(716) 272-1978, fax

Hickey, M. Christine, Esq.
719 E. Genesee St., Suite 225
Syracuse, NY 13210
(315) 422-9756, voice

Hinckley, Dolly
Divorce Mediation Associates
47 Round Trail Dr.
Pittsford, NY 14534
(716) 381-4841, voice
(716) 381-4841, fax

Huggins, Donna L.
Mediation Center of Rochester
2024 W. Henrietta Rd., Suite 5-G
Rochester, NY 14623
(716) 272-1990, voice
(716) 272-1978, fax

Keiser, Susan
149 Main St.
P.O. Box 350
Livingston Manor, NY 12758
(914) 439-5550, voice
(914) 439-5554, fax

Kimmelman, Donald M.
14 Balmville Lane
Newburgh, NY 12550-1422
(914) 561-1087, voice

Kingdom, Colleen A.
Ackerman Family/Divorce
  Mediation Center
130 Castlegrove Dr.
Rochester, NY 14612
(716) 225-2050, voice

Kleiman, Mark, JD
Community Mediation Services,
  Inc.
89-64 163rd St.
Queens, NY 11432
(718) 523-6868 #248, voice
(718) 523-8204, fax

Kuhn, Julie Z., MS, CSW
141 Euclid Ave.
Hastings-on-Hudson, NY 10706
(914) 478-1700, voice

Lazar, Kathryn S.
Mid-Hudson Divorce and Family
  Mediation
110 Rt. 82
Hopewell Junction, NY 12533
(914) 896-9651, voice

Levine, Barbara S., MSW CSW
2701 Rosendale Rd.
Schenectady, NY 12309
(518) 377-2802, voice

Lewin, Vicki
Goodman Associates
11 N. Goodman St.
Rochester, NY 14607
(716) 244-1600, voice
(716) 244-4135, fax

Lundquist, Jill, CSW
Mid-Hudson Divorce and Family
  Mediation
Wildey Road, P.O. Box 23
Barrytown, NY 12507
(914) 471-7167, voice

Marshall, Lorraine, MBA, JD
Law Offices of Lorraine Marshall
200 Mamaroneck Ave
White Plains, NY 10601
(914) 428-1040, voice
(914) 428-1595, fax

Marvald, Elizabeth H.
Mediation Center of Rochester
2024 West Henrietta Rd.,
  Suite 5-G
Rochester, NY 14623-1355
(716) 272-1990, voice
(716) 272-1978, fax

McClelland, Helvi, Esq.
Mediation Services
16 N. Goodman St., #113
Rochester, NY 14607
(716) 473-8723, voice
(716) 473-7711, fax

Miller, Marilyn A., Esq.
Attorney at Law
Mediator
1221 East Genesee St.
Syracuse, NY 13210
(315) 428-1221, voice

Miller, Mary N.
The Divorce and Family
  Resource Center
43-31 223rd St.
Queens, NY 11361
(718) 631-0156, voice
(718) 631-0154, fax

Milowe, Joan
3 Constitution Dr.
Glenmont, NY 12077
(518) 439-1314, voice

Neumann, Kenneth
Center for Family and Divorce
  Mediation
111 W. 90th St.
Townhouse B
New York, NY 10024
(212) 799-4302, voice
(212) 721-1012, fax

Niles, Robert C.
Dispute Mediation Program
51 Kenaware Ave.
Delmar, NY 12054
(518) 439-3404, voice

Norton, Nancy
26 Quarry Rd.
Ithaca, NY 14850
(607) 272-0556, voice

Pantaleo, Lorraine H., JD
Mediation Services
21 Hilltop Dr.
Chappaqua, NY 10514
(914) 238-5150, voice

Plesent, Emanuel, RCSW
Divorce Mediation Center of
  Long Island
340 A Willis Ave.
Mineola, NY 11501
(516) 747-1344, voice
(516) 747-4489, fax

Pope, Sally Ganong, MEd, JD
23 W. 73rd St.
New York, NY 10023
(212) 721-0770, voice
(212) 721-0773, fax

Potter, Barbara J.
Mediation Services Inc.
48 Dietz St., Suite I
Oneonta, NY 13820
(607) 433-1672, voice

Reid, Roger S.
Family Mediation Center
7000 E. Genesee St.
Building B
Fayetteville, NY 13066
(315) 446-5513, voice
(315) 446-5513, fax

Runfola, Ross T., JD, PhD
Director
Siegel, Kelleher & Kahn
Matrimonial Mediation Center
420 Franklin St.
Buffalo, NY 14202
(800) 888-5288, voice
(716) 885-3369, fax

Sanders-Demott, Jill
91 Hillside Dr.
Mahopac, NY 10541
(914) 621-1231, voice

Scher, Steve
82 Hart Blvd.
Staten Island, NY 10301
(718) 727-2901, voice

Shanok, Susan Whiting, NCPsyA,
    CTC
324 W. 22nd St., PH
New York, NY 10011
(212) 242-4194, voice
(212) 645-0392, fax

Shapiro, Deanna S., MS
RD #1, Box 728
Croton-on-Hudson, NY 10520
(914) 271-4947, voice

Shequine, Elizabeth K.
17 Collegeview Ave.
Poughkeepsie, NY 12603
(914) 471-2039, voice
(914) 486-4080, fax

Sloan, Sydell S., MA
17-26 215 St.
Queens, NY 11360
(718) 631-1600, voice
(718) 423-0325, fax

Stallman, Peggy, CSW
21 Carol Dr.
Mt. Kisco, NY 10549
(914) 666-6708, voice
(914) 666-6708, fax

Stillman, Philip
2781 Rosedale Rd.
Schenectady, NY 12309
(518) 370-4645, voice

Walker, Dolores Deane, JD, CSW
412 Avenue of the Americas,
    Suite 502
New York, NY 10011
(212) 691-6073, voice

Weiner, Judith, MA
10 Patricia Lane
White Plains, NY 10605
(914) 997-1222, voice

Yahm, Howard, CSW
Center for Family & Divorce
    Mediation
146 Willow Tree Rd.
Monsey, NY 10952
(914) 354-3158, voice
(212) 721-1012, fax

Yale, Diane, JD
The Mediation Alternative
4465 Douglas Ave., #10G
Bronx, NY 10471-3523
(718) 601-6265, voice
(718) 601-6455, fax

NORTH CAROLINA

Alschuler, Cathryn Fishman, MS,
EdD
Repay, Inc.
Catawba County Justice Center
P.O. Drawer 969
Newton, NC 28658
(704) 464-6744, voice

Bobo, Judith K.
Family Counseling & Mediation
108 W. Kime St.
Burlington, NC 27215
(919) 227-8412, voice

Bradley, Scott
Resolve! Associates
Mediation Network–North
Carolina
P.O. Box 282
Chapel Hill, NC 27514-0282
(919) 929-6333, voice
(919) 933-4465, fax

Cochran, Sherry M.
3216 Bedford Ave.
Raleigh, NC 27607
(919) 828-4001, voice

Cox, M. Susan, MSW, CCSW,
BCD
6821 Dumbarton Dr.
Charlotte, NC 28210
(704) 556-9030, voice

Green, Susan Falk
Carolina Mediation Assoc.
522 N. Elam Ave.
Greensboro, NC 27403
(910) 854-2391, voice
(910) 288-2102, fax

Hood, Jan
Administrative Offices of the
Court
P.O. Box 248
Raleigh, NC 28602
(919) 733-7107, voice
(919) 715-5779, fax

Kahn, Annette L., CCSW, BCD
25B Mount Bolus Rd.
Chapel Hill, NC 27514
(919) 967-1291, voice
(919) 967-3336, fax

Livermore, Jean Randle, CCSW
Counseling Services
18 W. Colony Place, #250
Durham, NC 27705
(919) 493-2674, x106, voice
(919) 493-1923, fax

Motsinger, John K.
Carolina Conciliation Services
Corp.
204 W. Cascade Ave.
Winston-Salem, NC 27127-2029
(910) 723-5900, voice
(910) 723-7711, fax

Neville, William G., EdD
10 Cogswood Rd.
Asheville, NC 28804
(704) 254-1058, voice
(704) 252-2180, fax

O'Briant, Celia, MEd, NCC
2711 D Pinedale Rd.
Greensboro, NC 27408
(919) 282-0052, voice

Price, George L.
603 Surry Rd.
Chapel Hill, NC 27514
(919) 942-6937, voice
(919) 942-6937, fax

Smith, Paul R.
The Mediation Center
189 College St.
Asheville, NC 28801
(704) 251-6089, voice
(704) 251-6061, fax

OHIO

Beaty, Janice A., MSSW
Crittenton Family Services
1414 E. Broad St.
Columbus, OH 43205
(614) 251-0103, voice
(614) 251-1177, fax

Blalock, Susan T.
2535 Brandon Rd.
Columbus, OH 43221
(614) 486-7200, voice

Brush, Sally
Beech Acres' Aring Institute
6881 Beechmont Ave.
Cincinnati, OH 45230
(513) 231-7205, x293, voice
(513) 624-0134, fax

Couch, Albert H., Jr.
Akron Family Mediation
150 N. Miller Rd., Bldg. 250A
Akron, OH 44333-3713
(216) 869-2818, voice
(216) 869-8113, fax

Damaser, Esther, PhD
Positive Perspectives
2355 Derr Rd.
Springfield, OH 45503
(513) 390-3800, voice

Dansker, Donna
Beech Acres' Aring Institute
6881 Beechmont Ave.
Cincinnati, OH 45230
(513) 231-7205, x297, voice
(513) 624-0134, fax

Doll, Barbara Thompson, MSW
Partners in Mediation
30 E. Central Pkwy., Suite 1200
Cincinnati, OH 45202
(513) 651-1010, voice
(513) 421-3455, fax

Eisenstein, Bette D.
Center for Family & Brief
    Therapy
24400 Highpoint Rd.
Beachwood, OH 44122
(216) 360-0776, voice
(216) 360-0358, fax

Frank, Sandra Hosmer
2137 Scottwood
Toledo, OH 43620
(410) 422-3711, voice

Green, Martha
Plowshares
12890 TWP Rd. 64
Glenford, OH 43739
(614) 659-2322, voice
(614) 659-2322, fax

Hill, Jane R., LISW
Jewish Family Service Assoc.
24075 Commerce Park
Beachwood, OH 44122
(216) 292-3999, voice
(216) 292-6313, fax

Hill, Marie
Beech Acres' Aring Institute
6881 Beechmont Ave.
Cincinnati, OH 45230
(513) 231-7205, x295, voice
(513) 624-0134, fax

Hulewat, Phyllis Drossin
Jewish Family Service Association
24075 Commerce Park Rd., #200
Cleveland, OH 44122
(216) 292-3999, voice
(216) 292-6313, fax

Johnson, Sandra G.
5480 E. Winding Way
Columbus, OH 43220
(216) 329-5290, voice

Kline, Annette E.
107 E. Spruce Avenue
Ravenna, OH 44266
(216) 296-1949, voice

Kolman, Marya Cody
Law Offices of Marya C. Kolman
731 E. Broad St.
Columbus, OH 43205
(614) 221-1058, voice
(614) 228-1135, fax

Kreiner, Cathleen E.
Private Compliant Mediations
  Service
911 Sycamore St.
Cincinnati, OH 45202
(513) 763-5130, voice
(513) 763-5032, fax

Lang, Michael D., JD
Antioch University
800 Livermore St.
Yellow Springs, OH 45387
(513) 767-6321, voice
(513) 767-6461, fax

Lansky, Dona T., PhD
3758 Clifton Ave.
Cincinnati, OH 45220
(513) 751-0392, voice
(513) 751-0392, fax

Larsen, Bea V.
30 Garfield Place, #920
Cincinnati, OH 45202
(513) 241-9844, voice
(513) 241-9908, fax

Lawson, Jerry H.
The Center for Resolution
  of Disputes
8 West 9th St.
Cincinnati, OH 45202
(513) 721-4466, voice
(513) 721-3383, fax

LeVine, Shoshana D., EdD,
  NCSP, PM
Behavioral Science Center, Inc.
2522 Highland Ave.
Cincinnati, OH 45219
(513) 221-8545, voice
(513) 861-2724, fax

Maxwell, Jennifer, PhD
Kent State University
Center for Peaceful Change
Kent, OH 44242
(216) 672-3143, voice

McColley, Denise Herman,
  MEd, JD
Maumee Valley Mediation
105 W. Main St.
Napoleon, OH 43545
(419) 599-5880, voice
(419) 599-2873, fax

Motz, Frank J.
Mediator
Belden Office Tower, Suite 213
4450 Belden Village St., N.W.
Canton, OH 44718
(216) 492-4004, voice

Petersen, Virginia, MSW
Divorce Services
Children's Hospital Guidance
  Centers
1704 Schrock Rd.
Columbus, OH 43229
(614) 794-2145, voice
(614) 794-6599, fax

Polanski, John, MEd
Mahoning County Domestic
  Relations Court
120 Market St.
Youngstown, OH 44503
(216) 740-2009, voice
(216) 740-2503, fax

Quinn, John R.
1006 Hatch St.
Cincinnati, OH 45202
(513) 579-1006, voice

Quinn, Maggie, JD, MSW
1006 Hatch St.
Cincinnati, OH 45202
(513) 579-1006, voice

Rauh, Trudy D.
Laufman, Rauh & Gerhardstein
617 Vine St.
1409 Enquirer Bldg.
Cincinnati, OH 45202-2422
(513) 621-9100, voice
(513) 345-5543, fax

Reed, Lou Ann W.
AAL Mediation
6726 Main St.
Newtown, OH 45244
(513) 271-4187, voice

Reis, Margaret A., Esq.
Partners in Mediation
30 E. Central Pkwy., Suite 1200
Cincinnati, OH 45202
(513) 651-1010, voice
(513) 421-3455, fax

Rundle, Jim
Crittenton Family Services
1414 E. Broad St.
Columbus, OH 43205
(614) 251-0103, voice
(614) 251-5305, fax

Slovin, Sherri Goren
30 Garfield Place, #920
Cincinnati, OH 45202
(513) 241-9844, voice
(513) 241-9908, fax

Solomon, Victoria E., JD, MSSA
11644 Canterbury Ave.
Pickering, OH 43147
(614) 575-4662, voice

Swift, Leslie H., PhD
1 Triangle Park Dr., #101
Sharonville, OH 45246
(513) 672-3500, voice
(513) 672-3503, fax

Thomas, Judith Wayne, PhD
Creative Resolutions
4 Sheppard Place
Granville, OH 43023
(614) 587-3367, voice
(614) 587-2798, fax

Wallace, Evelyn Marie
4039 Rose Hill Ave.
Cincinnati, OH 45229
(513) 281-8419, voice
(513) 281-0501, fax

OKLAHOMA

Hulett, Carrie S.
Horning, Johnson, Grove,
    Moore, Hulett, & Thompson
119 N. Robinson, #1100
Oklahoma City, OK 73102
(405) 232-3407, voice
(405) 232-3461, fax

Riley, Ann T., MSW, LCSW
110 N. Mercedes, Suite 400
Norman, OK 73069
(405) 366-6100, voice
(405) 366-8702, fax

OREGON

Atkin, Joe
1050-G Crater Lake Ave.
Medford, OR 97504
(503) 776-9166, voice

Bridges, Lynda
2040 Commercial St. S.E.
Salem, OR 97302
(503) 364-2016, voice
(503) 364-2585, fax

Bryen, Gloria S., MA
West Hills Counseling Center
14060 S.W. Maverick Ct.
Beaverton, OR 97008
(503) 644-1027, voice

Cohen, Stanley N., PhD
1119 N.W. 1st St.
Dundee, OR 97115-9537
(503) 538-7982, voice
(503) 538-7982, fax

Coleman, Ben
Ben Coleman Counseling
1698 Liberty St. S.E.
Salem, OR 97302
(503) 363-5487, voice
(503) 363-5487, fax

Corcoran, Kathleen O'Connell
The Mediation Center
440 E. Broadway, Suite 340
Eugene, OR 97401
(541) 484-9710, voice
(541) 345-4024, fax

Dixon, Pat, MS
Mediation Services
2695 12th Place S.E.
Salem, OR 97302
(503) 363-8075, voice
(503) 391-5348, fax

Etter, Jeanne, PhD
Teamwork for Children
85444 Teague Loop
Eugene, OR 97405
(503) 342-2692, voice
(503) 342-2692, fax

Gartland, John C., JD
Doyle Gartland Nelson &
    McCleery, P.C.
P.O. Box 11230
Eugene, OR 97440-3430
(503) 344-2174, voice
(503) 344-0209, fax

Gold, Lois, ACSW
Family Mediation Center
1020 SW Taylor, #650
Portland, OR 97205
(503) 248-9740, voice
(503) 295-0814, fax

Harding, Harold S.
Hal Harding Mediation Service
312 S.W. Jefferson
P.O. Box 1201
Corvallis, OR 97339
(503) 757-7594, voice
(503) 757-1310, fax

Juelfs, Larry
Clackamas County Family Court
    Service
704 Main St., #200
Oregon City, OR 97045
(503) 655-8414, voice
(503) 650-3584, fax

Kadish, Joshua D.
Meyer & Wyse
900 S.W. 5th Ave., #1900
Portland, OR 97204
(503) 228-8448, voice
(503) 273-9135, fax

Melamed, James, JD
The Mediation Center
440 E. Broadway, Suite 340
Eugene, OR 97401
(541) 345-1456, voice
(541) 345-4024, fax

Mounts, Kathleen A.
Common Ground Mediation
1033 Forrester Way
Eugene, OR 97401
(503) 342-2388, voice

Nolan, Barbara C.
Robinwood Center
19157 Willamette Dr.
West Linn, OR 97068
(503) 635-2123, voice

Oster, Warren
Clackamas County Juvenile Court
2121 Kaen Rd.
Oregon City, OR 97045
(503) 655-8342, voice
(503) 655-8448, fax

Reiman, John W., PhD
P.O. Box 474
Monmouth, OR 97361
(503) 753-4667, voice
(503) 838-8150, fax

Scher, Linda R.
Johnston & Root
1500 S.W. First Ave., #630
Portland, OR 97201
(503) 226-7986, voice
(503) 223-0743, fax

Silverman, Peter
111 Bush St.
Ashland, OR 97520
(503) 776-7171, x198, voice

Slezak, Ingrid
1000 S.W. Broadway, Suite 1710
Portland, OR 97205
(503) 223-2671, voice
(503) 223-0402, fax

Stouffer, Mary, LMFT
Clackamas County Family Court
    Service
19626 S. Ferguson Rd.
Oregon City, OR 97045
(503) 632-6670, voice

Taylor, Alison Y.
P.O. Box 1131
Hillsboro, OR 97123
(503) 640-0731, voice
(503) 640-0731, fax

Thurlow, Diane
217 Crest Dr.
Eugene, OR 97405
(503) 342-2388, voice

Warren, W. Suzanne, MS
Salem Mediation and Counseling
    Service
1764 37th Ave. N.W.
Salem, OR 97304
(503) 363-0316, voice
(503) 363-0316, fax

PENNSYLVANIA

Backlund, Winifred, MEd, NCC
2331 Merel Dr.
Hatfield, PA 19440
(215) 721-1813, voice
(215) 723-1211, fax

Blumstein, Edward, Esq.
Edward Blumstein & Associates
1518 Walnut St., 4th Floor
Philadelphia, PA 19102
(215) 790-9666, voice
(215) 790-1988, fax

Borke, Helene, PhD
6637 Aylesboro Ave.
Pittsburgh, PA 15217
(412) 421-6616, voice
(412) 421-6616, fax

Cohen, Nancy S., JD, PhD
1760 Market St., Suite 700
Philadelphia, PA 19103
(215) 575-9140, voice
(215) 386-1743, fax

Della Noce, Dorothy J., JD
160 Brochant Circle
Blue Bell, PA 19422
(215) 661-9755, voice
(215) 661-9756, fax

Emerick, Rebecca L., MS, MBA,
  CPA
Another Perspective Associates
1017 Mumma Rd., Suite 213
Wormleysburg, PA 17043
(717) 763-4882, voice
(717) 737-6286, fax

Gaber, Deborah, Esq.
528 N. Berks St.
Allentown, PA 18104
(610) 770-9308, voice
(610) 433-2993, fax

Goren, Sara Lee, Esq.
512 Bethlehem Park
Fort Washington, PA 19034
(215) 283-9913, voice
(215) 283-9934, fax

Hanna, Edward P., DSW
661 Reading Ave.
West Reading, PA 19611
(610) 373-5005, voice

Josephs, E. Sherle, MA
Mediation Masters
134 W. Lyndhurst Dr.
Pittsburgh, PA 15206
(412) 371-1000, voice
(412) 481-5601, fax

Kidd, Nancy Van Tries, MEd,
  DEd
Psychological and Mediation
  Resources
173 Indian Hill Rd.
Boalsburg, PA 16827
(814) 466-6666, voice
(814) 466-6699, fax

Klein, Don Stephen, Esq.
Lehigh Valley Mediation, Inc.
1436 Hampton Rd.
Allentown, PA 18104
(610) 395-7933, voice

Latman, Carrie C.
2130 Penn Ave.
West Lawn, PA 19609
(610) 678-4410, voice

Marcus, Patricia R., Esq.
145 E. Market St.
York, PA 17401
(717) 852-7272, voice
(717) 852-7360, fax

Mastros, Michael R.
Mediation Services
320 N. Duke St.
Lancaster, PA 17602
(717) 393-4440, voice
(717) 393-5506, fax

Riegler, Elliot, PhD
2151 Linglestown Rd., Suite 200
Harrisburg, PA 17110
(717) 540-1313, voice
(717) 540-1416, fax

Rubin, Fredric David, Esq.
2 Firewood Dr.
Holland, PA 18966
(215) 860-2525, voice
(215) 677-5131, fax

Shienvold, Arnold T., PhD
Central Pennsylvania Mediation
  Service, Inc.
2151 Linglestown Rd.
Suite 200
Harrisburg, PA 17110
(717) 540-9005, voice
(717) 540-1416, fax

Shopp, Judy
2935 Broxton Lane
York, PA 17402-3824
(717) 755-4224, voice
(717) 840-1455, fax

Sutton, Richard D., DMin
208 Stonybrook Dr.
Norristown, PA 19403
(610) 768-2154, voice
(610) 768-2470, fax

Wahrhaftig, Paul, JD
Divorce & Separation Mediation
  Center
7514 Kensington St.
Pittsburgh, PA 15221
(412) 371-1000, voice
(412) 481-5601, fax

Wisch, Patricia B., EdD
Mediation Services
1601 Walnut St., Suite 1424
Philadelphia, PA 19102
(215) 988-9104, voice

RHODE ISLAND

Bettigole, Bryna B.
29 Wilcox Ave.
Pawtucket, RI 02860
(401) 723-0353, voice

SOUTH CAROLINA

Bryan, Mary Lowndes
1528 Blanding St.
Columbia, SC 29201
(803) 252-5905, voice
(803) 748-9220, fax

Fields, Joyce W., PhD
Family Mediation Services
2212 Devine St.
Columbia, SC 29205
(803) 799-2323, voice

Hamrick, Diane David
655 St. Andrews Blvd.
Charleston, SC 29407
(803) 571-2040, voice
(803) 556-0701, fax

Harness, Cotton C., III
Ogletree, Deakins, Nash, Smoak
& Stewart
First Union Bldg.
177 Meeting St.
P.O. Box 1808
Charleston, SC 29402
(803) 853-1300, voice
(803) 853-9992, fax

Harness, Julie C.
Harness & Associates
11 49th Ave.
Isle of Palms, SC 29451
(803) 884-6473, voice

Hobbs, Sandra
117 Cove Court
Yacht Cove
Columbia, SC 29212
(907) 274-4211, voice

Melton, Barbara
Mediation Associates
171 Church St., Suite 300
Charleston, SC 29401
(803) 723-8002, voice
(803) 723-8002, fax

Smith, F. Glenn, JD, LMFT
Family Mediation Service
2212 Devine St.
Columbia, SC 29205
(803) 771-6107, voice
(803) 799-8249, fax

Upchurch, Donna Willson, PhD
1403½ Calhoun St.
Columbia, SC 29201
(803) 252-1866, voice

Young, Nancy M.
Dispute Resolution Services, Inc.
P.O. Box 8626
Columbia, SC 29202
(803) 799-7666, voice
(803) 252-3035, fax

SOUTH DAKOTA

Berget, J. Lee
P.O. Box 578
Sioux Falls, SD 57101
(605) 371-3017, voice

TENNESSEE

Barker, Ann, Esq.
8128 Chesterfield Dr.
Knoxville, TN 37909
(615) 694-4571, voice
(615) 694-9873, fax

Barton, Lynn P., LCSW
4535 Harding Rd., #102
Nashville, TN 37205
(615) 269-4557, voice

Burns, Margaret Devany, EdD, RN
Mediation Services of Oak Ridge,
  Inc.
1345 Oak Ridge Tpk., M350
Oak Ridge, TN 37830
(615) 481-3555, voice

Davis, Gregory S., MS
4933 Wise Hills Rd.
Knoxville, TN 37920
(615) 579-1356, voice
(615) 577-0561, fax

McMahan, Katherine
415 Georgia Ave.
Chattanooga, TN 37403
(615) 756-4653, voice
(615) 756-8120, fax

Redden, Jack, MA
4370 Fizer Cove
Memphis, TN 38117
(901) 682-3371, voice
(901) 763-3272, fax

Taylor, Virginia D., PhD
7134 Highway 100
Nashville, TN 37221
(615) 356-5343, voice

Wurzburg, Jocelyn Dan, JD
5118 Park Ave., Suite 232
Memphis, TN 38117-5708
(901) 684-1332, voice
(901) 684-6693, fax

Zaha, Mary Ann Peterson
Mediation Institute—Conflict
  Solutions
7400 River Ridge Dr.
Chattanooga, TN 37416-1092
(615) 877-3902, voice

TEXAS

Adams, Laury
Adams' Med. & Financial
  Resource Center
800 Gessner, #252
Houston, TX 77024-4256
(713) 465-2347, voice
(713) 468-4486, fax

Adams, Susanne C., MA
The Mediation Group, Inc.
2401 Turtle Creek Blvd.
Dallas, TX 75219
(214) 238-5050, voice
(214) 238-1499, fax

Anderson, Michael R., PhD
308 S. Third St.
Harlingen, TX 78550
(210) 425-8077, voice
(210) 425-8077, fax

Bean, Molly
2502 Barton Hills Dr.
Austin, TX 78704
(512) 476-3323, voice
(512) 476-0108, fax

Bryant, Suzanne
Mediator and Attorney at Law
1209 W. 5th St.
Austin, TX 78703-5255
(512) 476-4760, voice
(512) 476-4799, fax

Coffey, Pamela Whigham
Dispute Resolution Center
415 W. 8th St.
Amarillo, TX 79101
(806) 372-3381, voice
(806) 373-3268, fax

Dougherty, Judy Kurth
Family & Business Mediation
  Services
Dougherty & Dougherty
909 Kipling
Houston, TX 77006
(713) 521-9551, voice
(713) 521-9828, fax

Garber, Martha Ann
580 Denton Tap Rd., Suite 270
Coppell, TX 75019
(214) 247-4902, voice
(214) 304-0400, fax

Graul, Don West
Attorney at Law
4550 Post Oak Place, Suite 150
Houston, TX 77027
(713) 629-1416, voice
(713) 629-1433, fax

Greenstone, James L., EdD, JD
Leviton & Greenstone
6211 W. Northwest Hwy., Suite
  C-250
Dallas, TX 75225
(214) 361-0209, voice
(214) 361-6545, fax

Hack, Linda, MA, JD
P.O. Box 595314
Dallas, TX 75359
(214) 698-8307, voice
(214) 761-1851, fax

Hagen, William T., CPF
16010 Barkers Point, Suite 215
Houston, TX 77079
(713) 870-8020, voice
(713) 870-0850, fax

Hoffman, Carol May, CPA
Mediation and Law Center
4550 Post Oak Place, Suite 150
Houston, TX 77027
(713) 629-1416, voice
(713) 629-1433, fax

James, Paula
2905 San Gabriel St., #216
Austin, TX 78705
(512) 476-3400, voice
(512) 469-9867, fax

Kirkpatrick, Gary J., MA
Mediation Negotiation Training,
   Inc.
2401 Turtle Creek Blvd.
Dallas, TX 75219
(800) 888-8609, voice
(214) 328-9396, voice
(214) 328-9397, fax

Lee, Jeanne
Mediation and Law Center
4550 Post Oak Place, Suite 150
Houston, TX 77027
(713) 629-1416, voice
(713) 468-5043, fax

Leviton, Sharon
6211 W. Northwest Hwy., #2806
Dallas, TX 75225
(214) 361-0209, voice

Slaikeu, Karl A., PhD
1717 W. 6th St., #215
Austin, TX 78703
(512) 482-0356, voice
(512) 474-4645, fax

Twomey, Karen L.
1023 S. Fleishel
Tyler, TX 75701
(903) 592-8374, voice
(903) 592-5293, fax

Valentini, D. Gene
South Plains Dispute
   Resolution Center
P.O. Box 3730
Lubbock, TX 79452
(806) 762-8721, voice
(806) 765-9544, fax

Yingling, Lynelle C., PhD
570 E. Quail Run Rd.
Rockwall, TX 75087
(214) 771-9985, voice
(214) 772-3669, fax

UTAH

Downes, William W., Jr.
Winder & Haslam
175 W. 200 S., Suite 4000
Salt Lake City, UT 84101
(801) 322-2222, voice
(801) 532-3706, fax

Keck, Marcella L., JD
Accord Mediation
6914 S. 3000 E., #205
Salt Lake City, UT 84121
(801) 944-5400, voice
(801) 944-8761, fax

VERMONT

Barker, Jennifer
Middlebury Mediation Center
P.O. Box 735
Middlebury, VT 05753
(802) 388-3212, voice

Bernstein, Ellen
Conflict Resolution Associates
78 Central Ave.
South Burlington, VT 05403
(802) 658-2578, voice

Bryan, Lee W.
475 Tansy Hill
Stowe, VT 05672
(802) 253-4113, voice
(802) 253-9496, fax

Estey, Alice
Program Director
Mediation/Conflict Management
Woodbury College
660 Elm St.
Montpelier, VT 05602
(802) 229-0516, voice
(802) 254-7725, fax

Feldman-Fay, Susan E.
A Mediation Partnership
P.O. Box 321
Fairfax, VT 05454
(800) 564-6859, voice
(800) 849-6975, fax

Hollyday, Ellen D.
P.O. Box 528
Windsor, VT 05089-0528
(802) 436-2964, voice
(802) 436-2964, fax

Kennedy, Marianne, Esq.
RR #1, Box 2330
Arlington, VT 05250
(802) 375-9552, voice
(802) 375-9552, fax

Swaim, Nina
Box 65
Sharon, VT 05065
(802) 763-2208, voice
(802) 763-2238, fax

Terry, Susanne
Rd. 2, Box 175
St. Johnsbury, VT 05819
(802) 748-3512, voice
(802) 748-3512, fax

VIRGINIA

Asaro, Karen
Mediation Consultants of
 Tidewater
1117 Ewell Rd.
Virginia Beach, VA 23455
(804) 363-8225, voice

Bagnell, Jerome, MEd, MSW
Divorce Mediation Service
6104 Holly Arbor Court
Chester, VA 23831-7760
(804) 768-1000, voice
(804) 768-1010, fax

Beaty, Joe
Dispute Alternatives
101 E. Main St.
P.O. Box 87
Marion, VA 24354
(703) 783-7015, voice
(703) 782-9474, fax

Birdzell, Valerie F.
1504 Woodduck Rd.
Suffolk, VA 23433
(804) 363-8225, voice

Brown, Emily M., LCSW
Key Bridge Therapy & Mediation
 Center
1925 N. Lynn St., Suite 700
Arlington, VA 22209
(703) 528-3900, voice
(703) 524-5666, fax

Bumbaugh, Edwin C., MSW
Community Mediation Center
36 Southgate Court, Suite 102
Harrisonburg, VA 22801
(540) 434-0059, voice
(540) 574-0174, fax

Cullison, Alexander C.
Alternative Dispute Resolution
 Service
9341 Tovito Dr.
Fairfax, VA 22031
(703) 691-0403, voice
(703) 691-0403, fax

Dunning, C. Mark
Commonwealth Mediation
3374 Flint Hill Place
Woodbridge, VA 22192
(703) 497-7870, voice

Fairfield, Kathryn Stolzfus
303 Nations Bank Bldg.
Harrisonburg, VA 22801
(703) 432-6144, voice
(540) 532-0953, fax

Foskett, Kathy
6206 Sierra Court
Manassas, VA 22111
(703) 335-5827, voice

Gaughan, Lawrence D., JD
Family Mediation of Greater
 Washington
10300 Eaton Place, #310
Fairfax, VA 22030-2239
(703) 273-4005, voice
(703) 273-4006, fax

Hale, Linda D.
Institute for Conflict
 Management
3783 Center Way
Fairfax, VA 22033-2602
(703) 591-3800, voice
(703) 352-7714, fax

Hanson Eckles, Merri
Peninsula Mediation Center
P.O. Box 7135
Hampton, VA 23666
(804) 838-0148, voice
(804) 357-3481, fax

Hartmann-Harlan, Martha D., JD
915 Kingsland Rd.
Richmond, VA 23231
(804) 795-9283, voice

Hess, Susan A.
Community Mediation Center
36 Southgate Court, Suite 102
Harrisonburg, VA 22801-9668
(703) 434-0059, voice
(703) 434-0399, fax

Hubard III, Tazewell T., JD
125 St. Paul's Blvd., Suite 201
Norfolk, VA 23510
(804) 627-6120, voice
(804) 625-2161, fax

Jackson, Joanne Ades, BΛ, MEd
Sixteenth District Juvenile and
   Domestic Relations Court
411 East High St.
Charlottesville, VA 22901
(804) 979-7191, voice

Kavanagh, Vincent F., Jr.
301 Linden Court
Sterling, VA 20164
(703) 437-4147, voice

Koplan, Harriet
Northern Virginia Mediation
   Services
4103 Chain Bridge Rd.
Fairfax, VA 22032
(703) 993-3656, voice
(703) 934-5142, fax

Lohman, Mark R.
1 Village Green Circle
Charlottesville, VA 22905
(703) 442-9090, voice
(804) 977-2944, fax

Massey, A. Blanton, LLB, LLM,
   CFP
A. Blanton Massey & Assoc., P.C.
1119 Caroline St.
P.O. Box 240
Fredericksburg, VA 22404-0240
(703) 373-1818, voice
(703) 373-5306, fax

Mast, Ervin J., LCSW
8470 Brunger St.
Manassas, VA 22111
(703) 941-9008, voice
(703) 750-0621, fax

Moore, Catherine L., LCSW
P.O. Box 7107
Richmond, VA 23221-0107
(804) 355-5944, voice
(804) 355-9922, fax

Myricks, Noel
University of Maryland
2000 Golf Course Dr.
Reston, VA 22091
(301) 405-4007, voice
(703) 716-0193, fax

Rubin, Judy S.
Dispute Settlement Center
3608 Tidewater Center
Norfolk, VA 23509
(804) 625-9616, voice
(804) 627-1394, fax

Ruebke, Timothy J.
Community Mediation Center
36 Southgate Court
Harrisonburg, VA 22801
(540) 434-0059, voice
(540) 574-0174, fax

Samuelson, Deborah L.
Peninsula Mediation Center
P.O. Box 7135
Hampton, VA 23666
(804) 838-0148, voice
(804) 357-3481, fax

Shepherd, William J.
Bethlehem UMC/Mediation
   Services of Virginia
1861 Rosemont Lane
Hayes, VA 23072
(804) 642-5141, voice

Shevlin, Jerri
Conflict Resolutions
12476 Sweet Leaf Terrace
Fairfax, VA 22033
(703) 385-3383, voice

Sprowls, Jeffrey P., JD
Family Mediation of Northern
   Virginia
7918 Jones Branch Dr., Suite 600
McLean, VA 22102
(703) 918-4950, voice
(703) 918-4949, fax

Turman, Duke Conduff, MS, LPC
Counseling Associates of
   Southwest Virginia
2807 S. Main St.
Blacksburg, VA 24060
(703) 552-1402, voice
(703) 552-3428, fax

West, Dennis Michael
6356 Meeting House Way
Alexandria, VA 22312
(703) 256-2871, voice

Whittaker, Catherine M., PhD
Family Mediation Services of
   Roanoke
3959 Electric Rd.
Roanoke, VA 24018
(540) 772-3108, voice
(540) 774-6396, fax

Whittaker, Robert L.
Whittaker Mediation Associates
8716 Ruggles Rd.
Richmond, VA 23229
(804) 288-0796, voice
(804) 648-3115, fax

Zelinger-Casway, Robin, LCS PC
9401 Courthouse Rd., #201
Chesterfield, VA 23832
(804) 748-3250, voice

WASHINGTON

Bauer-Hughes, Jayne, MA, JD
Amicus Dispute Resolution
P.O. Box 337
South Bend, WA 98586
(800) 231-3422, voice
(360) 875-5290, voice

Bergquist, A. Bruce
203 4th Ave. E., #320
Olympia, WA 98501
(360) 705-1512, voice
(360) 956-1277, fax

Cockrill, Patrick R.
P.O. Box 487
Yakima, WA 98907
(509) 575-1500, voice
(509) 575-1227, fax

Dearborn, Susan
Pacific Family Mediation Institute
12505 Bel-Red Rd., #211
Bellevue, WA 98005
(206) 451-7940, voice
(206) 324-4945, fax

Eberle, Richard M.
Eberle Mediation Services
10900 N.E. 8th St., #900
Bellevue, WA 98004
(206) 454-0724, voice
(206) 450-9864, fax

Hatzenbeler, Mary J., MSW
316 E. 4th Plain Blvd.
Vancouver, WA 98663
(360) 695-6188, voice
(360) 737-7686, fax

Jeffers, Judith D., MA, JD
2600 Two Union Square
601 Union St.
Seattle, WA 98101-4000
(206) 292-9800, voice
(206) 340-2563, fax

Kaplan, Nancy, MSW
CRU-Conflict Resolution
    Unlimited
845 106th Ave. N.E., Suite 109
Bellevue, WA 98004
(206) 451-4015, voice
(206) 451-1477, fax

Mahaffy, Samuel G.
Northwest Mediation Associates
    Inc.
523 W. 18th St.
Spokane, WA 99203
(208) 667-5389, voice
(208) 263-7353, fax

Rofkar, Barbara A.
Family Mediation Services
1155 N. State St., #524
Bellingham, WA 98225
(206) 671-6416, voice

Schweinfurth, Ruth B.
Attorney at Law
844 Fern Court
Walla Walla, WA 99362
(509) 525-2539, voice

Smith, Pamela
18611 68th Street E.
Bonny Lake, WA 98390
(206) 863-9653, voice

Stipe, Sue A., MS
33919 9th Ave. S., #201
Federal Way, WA 98003
(206) 467-1722, x1489, voice

Wilburn, Donnelly J.
2815 130th Place N.E.
Bellevue, WA 98005
(206) 453-8452, voice
(206) 637-9541, fax

WASHINGTON, D.C.

Lesser, Roger
Center for Mediation
1666 Connecticut Ave. N.W.,
 Suite 250
Washington, DC 20009
(202) 797-7999, voice
(202) 797-2354, fax

Maida, Peter R., PhD, JD
6242 29th St. N.W.
Washington, DC 20015
(202) 362-2515, voice
(202) 362-2515, fax

WISCONSIN

Ackerman, Marc J., PhD
North Shore Psychotherapy
 Assoc.
250 West Coventry Court,
 Suite 209
Milwaukee, WI 53217-3966
(414) 351-0066, voice
(414) 351-6772, fax

Costrini-Norgal, Rita
Rock County Mediation and
 Family
51 South Main St.
Janesville, WI 53545
(608) 757-5549, voice

Dernbach, Barbara
Try Mediation
Eau Claire County Courthouse
721 Oxford Ave., Room #2570
Eau Claire, WI 54703
(715) 839-6295, voice
(715) 839-6243, fax

Greenlee, Rebecca E., MSSW, JD
Attorney at Law
P.O. Box 5086
Madison, WI 53705
(608) 238-7122, voice
(608) 238-9606, fax

Hamann, John B., EdD
The Mediation Center
710 N. Main, Box 405
River Falls, WI 54022
(715) 425-9558, voice
(715) 425-1055, fax

Hamann, Stephanie Marie, MSE
The Mediation Center
710 N. Main, Box 405
River Falls, WI 54022
(715) 425-9558, voice
(715) 425-1055, fax

Hampton, Marilyn
3002 Begonia St.
Wausau, WI 54401-1861
(715) 847-5723, voice

Milne, Ann L., ACSW
Association of Family and
  Conciliation Courts
329 W. Wilson St.
Madison, WI 53703-3612
(608) 251-0604, voice
(608) 251-2231, fax

Salem, Peter
Association of Family and
  Conciliation Courts
329 W. Wilson St.
Madison, WI 53703-3612
(608) 251-4001, voice
(608) 251-2231, fax

Wylie, John G.
Patterson, Jensen, Wylie, Silton &
  Seifert
331 E. Washington St.
Appleton, WI 54911
(414) 739-2366, voice
(414) 739-8893, fax

WYOMING

Whitfield-Weinbrandt, J. C.
Skyline Ranch, Box 20
100 W. Ridge Rd.
Jackson Hole, WY 83001
(307) 733-7206, voice

ALBERTA

Amundson, Jon K., PhD
Amundson and Assoc.
2003 14th St. N.W., #206
Calgary, AB T2M 3N4
Canada
(403) 289-2511, voice

Andrew, Patricia Mary
Northland Family Counseling
  Centre Ltd.
10508 82nd Ave., #201
Edmonton, AB T6E 2A4
Canada
(403) 439-5683, voice
(403) 439-5679, fax

Dimirsky, Mark, PhD
Systemics Behavioral Services,
   Ltd.
4808 Ross St., #508
Red Deer, AB T4N 1X5
Canada
(403) 347-1500, voice
(403) 342-1150, fax

Flatters, Nancy A., BA, LLB
777 8th Ave. S.W., #2100
Calgary, AB T2P 3R5
Canada
(403) 265-7777, voice
(403) 269-8911, fax

Fong, Larry Sun, PhD
Fong & Associates
736 6th Ave. S.W., Suite 850
Calgary, AB T2P 3T7
Canada
(403) 233-7533, voice
(403) 266-4998, fax

Kushner, Margo Anne, MSW
Impacts Consulting Ltd.
908 17th Ave. S.W., #315
Calgary, AB T2T 0A3
Canada
(403) 245-8787, voice
(403) 229-2647, fax

McKay, Joanne
McKay Mediation Services
305 Parkland Square
4901–48 St.
Red Deer, AB T4N 6M4
Canada
(403) 347-7020, voice
(403) 343-0251, fax

Taylor, Kent, PhD
7503 110th Ave.
Edmonton, AB T5B 0A2
Canada
(403) 427-8329, voice

BRITISH COLUMBIA

Ellison, Cam
General Delivery
Roberts Creek, BC V0N 2W0
Canada
(604) 253-8090, voice
(604) 253-8090, fax

Johnson, Ellen
The Family Mediation Services
   Society of B.C.
13401 108th Ave., #1800
Surrey, BC V3T 5T4
Canada
(604) 589-9090, voice
(604) 589-2130, fax

NOVA SCOTIA

Starnes, Susannah, LLB
AMS Mediation Associates
1568 Hollis St., Suite 220
Halifax, NS B3J 1V3
Canada
(902) 422-3681, voice
(902) 422-5519, fax

Strug, Annette, MSW, RSW
1568 Hollis St., Suite 220
Halifax, NS B3J 1V3
Canada
(902) 422-3681, voice
(902) 422-5519, fax

ONTARIO

Fitz, Jacqueline Hoffman
390 Wellesley St., Suite 21
Toronto, ON M4X 1H6
Canada
(416) 922-0928, voice

Landau, Barbara, PhD, LLB,
 LLM
137 Sheppard Ave. E.
Willowdale, ON M2N 3A6
Canada
(416) 223-5111, voice
(416) 223-5359, fax

Ryan, Judith P., MSW, LLB, LLM
12 Birch Ave., Suite 207
Toronto, ON M4C 1V8
Canada
(416) 928-1154, voice
(416) 925-6684, fax

QUEBEC

Shaposnick, Philip
The Interlex Group
3680 Dela Montagne St.
Montreal, PQ H3G 2A8
Canada
(514) 289-8614, voice
(514) 289-8774, fax

SASKATCHEWAN

Acton, Kenneth W.
Saskatchewan Justice Mediation
   Services
2151 Scarth St.
Regina, SK S4P 3V7
Canada
(306) 787-5749, voice
(306) 787-0088, fax

Hamoline, Daniel L., MSW, LLB
Fifth Avenue Mediation &
   Counselling
215–728 Spadina Crescent E.
Saskatoon, SK S7K 4H7
Canada
(306) 653-2599, voice
(306) 653-2523, fax

Jacques, John D., PAg
Mediation Services
2151 Scarth St.
Regina, SK S0C 2C0
Canada
(306) 787-5747, voice
(306) 787-0088, fax

Ramsay, Brent W.
Cardwell Human Resources
200–333 25th St. E.
Saskatoon, SK S7K 0L4
Canada
(306) 242-1010, voice
(306) 242-0101, fax

Walter, Barbara
Mediation Services
Saskatchewan Justice
385 Powell Crescent
Swift Current, SK S9H 4L7
Canada
(306) 787-5747, voice
(306) 778-3389, fax

INTERNATIONAL

Bowen, Donald J., BA, BSc, BSW,
   MLitt
P.O. Box 672
Epping
Sydney 2121
Australia
02-622-0522, voice

Brandon, Meike
Relationships Australia
159 St. Paul's TCE
Brisbane, Queensland 4000
Australia
07-831-2005, voice
07-832-4864, fax

Brown, Henry J.
58 Greenham Rd.
Muswell Hill
London N1O 1LP
England
081-365-2280, voice

Charlesworth, Stephanie, BA,
    MA, LLB
86 Lang St.
North Carlton, VIC 3054
Australia
(03) 387-3352, voice
(03) 347-0685, fax

Corry, Geoffrey
Athena Mediation
95 Stillorgan Wood
Stillorgan
Co. Dublin
Ireland
(353-1) 288-4190, voice
(353-1) 288-4190, fax

Garwood, Fiona
Family Mediation Scotland
127 Rose Street, S. Lane
Edinburgh EH2 5BB
Scotland
011-441-31-220-1610, voice
011-441-31-220-6895, fax

Murphy, Maura Wall
2 Shanganahg Vale
Loughlinstown
Co. Dublin
Ireland
01-2824026, voice

Parkinson, Lisa, MA CQSW
Family Mediators Assoc.
The Old House Rectory Gardens
Bristol BS10 7AQ
England
01179 500140, voice

Prunty, Geraldine
241 Blackhorse Ave.
Dublin 7
Ireland
377755, x3940, voice

Williams, Michael
14 Charleville Rd.
Rathmines
Dublin 6
Ireland
01135314978402, voice
01135314978402, fax

Zaidel, Susan, PhD
10 Koyfman St.
Haifa 34780
Israel
04-256-123, voice

Some Helpful Books

MEDIATION

Bush, Robert A. Baruch, and Joseph P. Folger. *The Promise of Mediation.* San Francisco: Jossey-Bass, 1994.

Coogler, O. J. *Structured Mediation in Divorce Settlement.* Lexington, Mass.: Lexington Books, 1978.

Erickson, Stephen, and Marilyn Erickson. *Family Mediation Casebook: Theory and Process.* New York: Brunner Mazel, 1988.

Folberg, Jay, and Alison Taylor. *Mediation: A Comprehensive Guide to Resolving Conflicts Without Litigation.* San Francisco: Jossey-Bass, 1984.

————, and Ann Milne. *Divorce Mediation: Theory and Practice.* New York: The Guilford Press, 1988.

Friedman, Gary. *A Guide to Divorce Mediation: How to Reach a Fair Legal Settlement at a Fraction of the Cost.* New York: Workman Publishing Co., 1993.

Haynes, John. *Fundamentals of Family Mediation.* Albany: State University of New York Press, 1994.

Haynes, John, and Gretchen Haynes. *Mediating Divorce: Casebook of Strategies for Successful Family Negotiation.* San Francisco: Jossey-Bass, 1989.

Irving, Howard. *Divorce Mediation: The Rational Alternative.* New York: Universe Books, 1980.

Johnston, Janet, and Linda Campbell. *Impasses of Divorce: The Dynamics and Resolution of Family Conflict.* New York: The Free Press, 1988.

Kressel, Kenneth, Dean G. Pruitt, and Associates. *Mediation Research.* San Francisco: Jossey-Bass, 1988 (© 1989).

Lemmon, John Allen. *Family Mediation Practice.* New York: Macmillan, 1985.

Mnookin, Robert, and L. Kornhauser. "Bargaining in the Shadow of the Law: The Case of Divorce." *Yale Law Journal* 960, 1979.

Moore, Christopher. *The Mediation Process: Practical Strategies for Resolving Conflict.* San Francisco: Jossey-Bass, 1986.

Neumann, Diane. *Divorce Mediation: How to Cut the Cost and Stress of Divorce.* New York: Henry Holt & Co., 1989.

Saposnek, Donald. *Mediating Child Custody Disputes: A Systematic Guide for Family Therapists, Court Counselors, Attorneys and Judges.* San Francisco: Jossey-Bass, 1983.

PARENTING

Ahrons, Constance. *The Good Divorce: Keeping Your Family Together When Your Marriage Comes Apart.* New York: HarperCollins, 1994.

Baris, Mitchell, Ph.D., and Carla Garrity, Ph.D. *Children of Divorce: A Developmental Approach to Residence and Visitation.* Asheville, N.C.: Psytec, 1988.

Blume, Judy. *It's Not the End of the World.* New York: Bantam Books, 1977 (© 1975).

Boegehold, Betty. *Daddy Doesn't Live Here Anymore.* New York: Golden Books, 1985.

Bonkowski, Sara, Ph.D. *Kids Are Non-Divorceable.* Chicago, Ill.: Buckley Publications, 1987.

Brown, Laurene, and Mark Brown. *Dinosaurs Divorce: A Guide for Changing Families.* New York: Little, Brown, 1986.

Cohen, Miriam. *Joint Custody Handbook.* Philadelphia: Running Press, 1991.

Folberg, Jay. *Joint Custody and Shared Parenting,* 2nd ed. New York: The Guilford Press, 1991.

Gardner, Richard, M.D. *The Boys' and Girls' Book About Divorce.* New York: Bantam Books, 1988.

Goff, Beth. *Where Is Daddy?* Boston: Beacon Press, 1985.

Hodges, William F. *Interventions for Children of Divorce.* New York: John Wiley, 1986.

Klein, Norma. *It's Not What You Expect.* New York: Avon Books, 1974 (© 1973).

———. *Taking Sides.* New York: Avon Books, 1976.

Lansky, Vicki. *Divorce Book for Parents: Helping Your Children Cope with Divorce and Its Aftermath.* New York: Penguin (Signet), 1991.

Ricci, Isolina, Ph.D. *Mom's House, Dad's House: Making Shared Custody Work.* New York: Collier Books, 1980.

Rofes, Eric, ed. *The Kids' Book of Divorce: By, For and About Kids.* New York: Vintage Books, 1982 (© 1981).

Stinson, Kathy. *Mom and Dad Don't Live Together Anymore*. Toronto: Annick Press, 1989.

Virtue, Doreen. *My Kids Don't Live with Me Anymore: Coping with the Custody Crisis*. Minneapolis: CompCare Publishers, 1988.

Wallerstein, Judy, and Joan Kelly. *Surviving the Breakup: How Children and Parents Cope with Divorce*. New York: Basic Books, 1980.

Wallerstein, Judy, and Sandra Blakeslee. *Second Chances: Men, Women & Children a Decade After Divorce, Who Wins, Who Loses, and Why*. New York: Ticknor & Fields, 1989.

Watson, Jane, R. Switzer, and J. Hirschberg. *Sometimes a Family Has to Split Up*. New York: Crown Publishers, 1988.

Willhoite, Michael. *Daddy's Roommate*. Boston: Alyson Publishers, 1990.

MISCELLANEOUS

Tannen, Deborah. *You Just Don't Understand*. New York: William Morrow, 1990.

Trafford, Abigail. *Crazy Time: Surviving Divorce and Building a New Life*, rev. ed. New York: HarperCollins, 1992.

Vaughan, Diane. *Uncoupling: Turning Points in Intimate Relationships*. New York: Vintage Books, 1990.

Woodhouse, Violet. *Divorce and Money*. Berkeley, Calif.: Nolo Press, 1992.

Index

sole proprietorship, 47
Structured Mediation in Divorce Settlement (Coogler), 97
substance abuse, 16, 23–24, 25, 48, 59
support payments:
  for alimony, 14, 48, 59
  for college education, 12, 46, 51, 56
  custodial accounts for, 44, 46, 52
  duration of payments for, 12, 74
  employment changes and, 12, 51
  future adjustments in, 51
  insurance coverage and, 13, 44
  mediation session on, 11–12, 115
  mediator's expertise on, 44, 49
  refusal of payments for, 49, 60
  state guidelines for, 11–12, 44, 49, 51, 60
  tax consequences for, 12, 44, 48, 51–52, 59

Tannen, Deborah, 95
taxation:
  age-55 exclusion advantages for, 57
  alimony deductability for, 14, 48, 59
  for apartment occupants, 53
  on capital gains, 13, 44, 46, 47, 52
  child support payments and, 12, 44, 51–52
  correct information on returns for, 15, 16
  mediator's expertise on, 51–52, 53, 55, 59, 84, 85

for pensions and retirement plans, 53
property division and, 44, 45, 52
for self-employment, 47, 56–57
team mediation, 81–83, 107–108, 129
tenant/landlord disagreements, community mediation for, 67
therapists:
  family mediation practices of, 78–79, 107
  mediators referred by, 64–65
  on stages of divorce process, 2
Triple A (American Arbitration Association), 66, 76
trusts, 47, 57

Udell, Laurie S., 117
Unitarian Universalist clergy, 68
unmarried couples, mediation services for, 112, 117

violence, domestic, 24, 26–31, 48, 60, 83
visitation agreements, 11
  see also child custody

wage assignments, 49, 74
Walters, Susan Sprague, 117
War of the Roses, 52
woman's advocate, 28

Yellow Pages, mediation services listed in, 2, 64
You Just Don't Understand (Tannen), 95

Diane Neumann
Divorce Mediation Srvcs.
Framingham, MA
(508) 879-9095

Advance Praise for *Choosing a Divorce Mediator*

"Ms. Neumann's book is an excellent resource for the public, the first of its kind, that succinctly defines the field of competent divorce mediation. It offers a way for divorcing couples to seek the highest quality mediator for their needs by its step-by-step process of questions to ask and issues to consider. It is long overdue in the field of mediation."
> —Stephen K. Erickson,
> director of the Erickson Mediation Institute

"This book is a major contribution to the field of mediation and is not only about choosing a mediator but also what mediation is all about. The best kept secret about divorce is revealed in the book—that divorce mediation is a viable alternative to the adversarial process, especially when couples choose competent mediators. Every divorcing couple should buy this before consulting with any professional about divorce."
> —Marilyn S. McKnight,
> director of Cooperative Solutions, Inc.

"This book is a welcome and important addition to the mediation literature. In a lively, engaging, easy to read style, Diane Neumann draws examples from her own practice, as well as those of her trainees and colleagues, to illustrate what clients should know when choosing a mediator. There is no other book that addresses this issue. Potential mediation clients will be extremely well served by this excellent resource."
> —Lynn Carp Jacob,
> past president of the Academy of Family Mediators

"For lawyers, mediators, other helping professionals and clients who need some clarification into the important areas of mediation, Diane Neumann provides personal insights about the most important issues. An invaluable guide to the process of divorce mediation."

—Larry S. Fong, Ph.D.,
past president of Family Mediation Canada

"A powerful survival guide for preventing your divorce from escalating to World War III! This book will rescue you from the confusing legal process and help you and your children minimize the emotional and financial stresses."

—Constance Ahrons, Ph.D.,
director of the Marriage & Family Therapy Program
and professor of sociology at the University
of Southern California